Peggy,

God richly bless you
in the reading of this book!

[signature]

Time Spent With God

Time Spent With God

Sandy Blackburn

HOPPER HERITAGE SERIES

Woodland Press, LLC

WOODLAND GOSPEL PUBLISHING
A division of Woodland Press, LLC
PUBLISHED IN THE USA

Acknowledgements

God the Father

Jesus the Son

and to the Holy Spirit dwelling in me

Dedicated to Deric, my husband; Pat McKim, my life coach; Joyce Hopper, my divine connector; Ms. Virginia Hopper Steele, my most special friend; Grandma Kirkman, my mentor. And to Penny York for the title, my family, and especially my grandchildren—Miranda, Zachary, and Ashleigh—who provided so much material.

Copyright © 2010 Sandy Blackburn

ISBN 978-0-9824939-8-4

SAN: 2 5 4 – 9 9 9 9

Foreword

Sandy Blackburn is a remarkable woman. She is devoted to the Lord Jesus Christ with vision, faith, and humility. She has honored me to write this Foreword to her book of devotional writings. It is a privilege thus to pay my respects to one of the most vital Christian women that I know.

God has given her one of His most gracious gifts by enabling her to write about everyday happenings in life. Nothing seems to be left out, the early morning sunrise, the birds of the air, her little stray cat, Boots of Grace, and people.

God teaches her through the insights of everyday life experiences and from her heart and hand flow these wonderful writings that we can all be inspired by and relate to. Sandy is sensitive to the Holy Spirit through her writings, witnessing, prayers, and speaking. She has the joy unspeakable and full of glory.

She has faced tragedy in her life through the loss of three beautiful young granddaughters in a terrible automobile accident. Also, she has some health issues and suffers with pain almost continually, but the Lord is her strength and comfort.

I know your hearts will be blessed and your relationships with the Lord will be deepened by Sandy's devotionals. Like Paul, she exemplifies his words, "This one thing I do, forgetting those things which are behind, I press on toward the mark for the prize of the high calling of God in Christ Jesus." (*Philippians 3:13, 14*)

— Virginia Hopper Steele

Introduction

For too many years I've been pregnant with the Word of God and allowing it to grow inside me through the Holy Spirit's revelation and empowerment. Most pregnancies last a mere nine months ... this one has drug on far too long. I know beyond a doubt that it's time to give birth to all that God, in His infinite grace, has revealed to me. This birthing process has been very labor intensive and I know that the pangs of labor pains will have all been worthwhile when I see the finished fruit.

Just like Paul and a new mother with her newborn bundle, I forget all that lies behind and look forward to the path ahead. As Mary sat at Jesus' feet, so have I been allowed that sacred privilege for the past five years. At the Master's feet, the Holy Spirit guides the dialogue and the revelation; the Holy Spirit quickens and empowers the interpretation. The Spirit enables this servant the gift of manifesting or making real God's Word to flesh and life experiences. Therein lies my interpretation of this endeavor as a pregnancy and childbirth.

This gift from God is not merely for me, but for those to whom it speaks. Our gifts and our blessings are for those around us, not just ourselves. These writings have been God's word to me and should they bless you also, they are words He wishes me to share. God in His glorious wisdom has watered His word seed on the inside of me with the living waters of His precious Son. This whole conception, pregnancy, and birth have been completely and totally a loving act from a most gracious God to this servant girl. My only part in this whole process has been to make the choice to spend time with Him, pick up my pen, and become His ready scribe ... *to God be ALL the glory!*

— **Sandy Blackburn**

"A powerful collection of writings that will both encourage and inspire."

— **Connie Hopper,** of The Hoppers

"Time Spent With God will surely take you on an intimate spiritual journey. We encourage you to get onboard."

— **Claude Hopper**, of The Hoppers

Table of Contents

1

A Foot Soldier

"'...Come let us go over to the garrison of these uncircumcised; it may be that the LORD will act for us; for nothing can hinder the LORD from saving by many or by few.' His armor bearer said to him, 'Do all that your mind inclines to. I am with you; as your mind is, so is mine'...Then Jonathan climbed up on his hands and feet, with his armor-bearer following after him. The Philistines fell before Jonathan, and his armor-bearer, coming after him, killed them..." (1 Samuel 14: 6-15).

Often, God reminds me that I'm simply a foot soldier. Any soldier must be protected and armed to be effective. My days are exciting and filled with opportunities abounding in the streets and byways of life. From the aisles of a Dollar Tree, drug store, or grocery store, to the tables of neighborhood restaurants, God brings opportunity and needs into His abundant and full life for me. Removing the scales from my eyes to see His hand and opportunity in my life has been an ongoing journey, process and blessings beyond my deserving.

Daily, God has allowed me the wisdom to put on His whole armor (Ephesians 6). It's His armor, not mine. Much like the shepherd boy David felt, when he tried to wear the armor of Saul before killing Goliath, the fit is beyond my comfort zone or capabilities. God is God and I am not; I pray each morning. Again, I repeat, I don His armor daily, not mine. Through the years, God, in His wisdom, has revealed to me that His armor took on a fleshly fit when He sent His Son, Jesus. In Him, the armor takes on a whole new reality to this particular foot soldier. It fits Jesus to a tee and when I am in Him and He is in me, the armor of God fits!

I fasten His belt of truth around my waist. Jesus is the way, the truth, and life everlasting; God's Word says so. I put on His breastplate of righteousness. I am the righteousness of God, in Christ Jesus; God's Word says so. For shoes for my feet, I put on whatever it will take to proclaim the gospel of peace. Jesus is the Prince of Peace; God's Word says so. I pick up the shield of faith with which to quench the fiery darts of the evil one for my battle is not against flesh and blood but against evil. My faith is in Jesus, Who overcame the devil and shines His light into the darkness that I might recognize evil wherever it rears its ugly head. Good overcomes evil. God's Word says so. I put on the helmet of salvation. My salvation is in Jesus; His atoning blood and the sacrifice He paid for me. He lived the life I cannot live, died the death I deserved, and rose again that I might be reconciled with God and have life abundant, God's Word says so. And finally, I wield the sword of the Spirit, which is the Word of God. Jesus is the Living Word. God's Word says so.

It's Jesus that I put on every morning. Jesus is God's armor that will equip us to fight our daily battle with the evil one. Just as the armor is His, not ours, so the battle is His, not ours. The Word of God tells us that Jesus fought that battle and won. He has already paid the price and crushed Satan under His heel. Again, the battle is won! That evil liar and deceiver would want us to believe that it's our fight but in reality, it's not. Our life isn't about us; it's about God. The one known as the Accuser would torment us and have us believe that we've lost. That is the furthest thing from God's Truth! God's Word says so!

Just as Jonathan's armor-bearer followed Jonathan into battle in the above Scripture, we need to have his heart when he said, "I am with you, as your mind is, so is mine" (I Samuel 4:6). Christ-centered thinking and actions will guarantee victory in this life. Just as Jonathan did, Jesus Christ will go ahead and we should follow like that trusting armor bearer. As the Philistines fell before Jonathan and the armor bearer followed his master, so we, too, should follow the Christ and allow Him to lay our enemies at our feet. It's His battle and He's already won, so follow Him into battle today with the confidence of this armor bearer in I Samuel.

Put on His armor, foot soldier! Put on Jesus and follow Him where He might lead today. The battle is won and, praise God, we're on the winning side!

2

A New Song

"I waited patiently for the LORD; He inclined to me and heard my cry. He drew me up from the desolate pit, out of the miry bog, and set my feet upon a rock, making my steps secure. He put a new song in my mouth, a song of praise to our God. Many will see and fear, and put their trust in the LORD" (Psalm 40:1-3).

Repeatedly I've written and shared about something that never ceases to amaze me. So many times I've awakened in the morning with a song rattling around in my brain, a song praising and worshiping God, of all things. It's there popping out in verbal choruses, and then it will recede back into the inner depths of my soul, only to pop up again when my mind wanders back to that place of oneness with my Creator and Lord.

Many is the morning whenever this occurs, that I finally give in to the song in my heart, and spend my time with God in songs of worship and praise. These devotional times always leave me refreshed and strengthened for the new day ahead. When I've finished my worship time, I regret not starting each and every day in just such a way. Time sometimes doesn't allow for this special beginning of the day. Urgent prayer requests, intercessory prayer, and prayers of thanksgiving should always give way to prayers of praise and worship, which sometimes take the form of songs. The Bible tells us that God inhabits the praises of His people.

I've never waited patiently for anything as the above Scripture describes. I do know that God hears my cries. I do know that he draws me near, delivers me, and sets my feet upon a rock. That rock has a name and its name

4

is Jesus. I know that my steps are indeed secure and that Jesus will walk each step with me no matter how dangerous or uncertain. As I continue to literally translate the above Scripture to myself, I can see that just maybe that song that God often puts in my heart and mouth are to show me that I am putting my trust in Him and that all fear has fled.

It's very difficult and nearly impossible to be fearful when you sing praise and worship songs. The Psalms have always brought me such comfort in times of need. As I reflect this morning, I'm reminded of the fact that the Psalms are equivalent to songs written in praise and worship. God has used song to minister to me more times than not. Song is a tool as much as faith, obedience, and the Word. Song can be used for our good. Song can lift us out of those miry bogs and set our feet upon THE ROCK.

John Wesley knew the importance of song when he prefaced the Methodist hymnals. Grab a hymnal some day and read the preface. Be a "real Christian," as Wesley said, and find hymns that you can sing that will witness of your Christian experience. Sing of how you have been lifted up. Sing with confidence and know that when you sing the song God put in your heart and mouth that you are singing to the One God who deserves all your praise and worship. He revels in your song to Him, and will refresh you and strengthen you in your deepest time of need.

Worship Him, praise Him, and forever sing that new song to Him. He alone is worthy. To God be all the praise and glory our heart songs can sing.

3

A Wound So Deep

"Praise the LORD! How good it is to sing praises to our God; for He is gracious, and a song of praise is fitting. The LORD builds up Jerusalem; He gathers the outcasts of Israel. He heals the broken-hearted, and binds up their wounds" (Psalms 147:1-3).

We all have scars. I don't mean the kind that can be seen on our bodies from scrapes and cuts that we've endured. Those scars that whelp up the skin and remind us of some past hurt, surgery, or accident are painless, and show us that the body is wondrously designed to heal itself whenever wounded. God did, indeed, do a miracle work when He engineered a body for us that can heal itself. As the Scripture tells us, "We are fearfully and wonderfully made" (Psalm 139:14).

We all have unseen scars. I mean those emotional and spiritual kinds, that form from past hurts or losses that we all must endure if we are to live life as intended. If we dare to love, we will eventually be wounded. It begins as a small child with friendships gone awry or a small pet that gets hit by a car. Later comes lost love or death of a grandparent or someone close to us. Whatever the wound, the hurt is real and must heal to form a scar that we can later utilize to face life.

Scars are necessary in order to deal with oncoming wounds. Wounds will come, in whatever form, to each and everyone of us. Wounds of disappointment, wounds of loss, wounds of pain, that will heal and eventually build our character into whomever we are to become. I'm amazed to look around and find that some of the most influential people I know are scarred with past wounds deeper than I could possibly face.

The key to overcoming is to allow a wound to become a scar. Some wounds might be so deep that the healing process takes longer than most. Some wounds might be so deep that only God's promise to bind them up will heal the brokenhearted. I'm positive that a divinely bound wound will eventually heal. That assurance allows me to sing praises to God as this Psalm describes. Praises befitting a God who knows first hand the pain of a wound so deep that it stretched into eternity are possible. I sing those praises today with bound wounds that will eventually heal.

Thank you, LORD God, for soaking those bindings with the love of Christ. Thank you, LORD God, that by Jesus' wound so deep, I am healed. Thank you for the healing balm of love that is saturated in each binding. Bind my broken heart, LORD. Bind my wound so tightly that Your divine healing process will take place, leaving a scar in place of a wound so deep. Thank you, LORD God, for all Your goodness and mercy. To You I sing praises today.

4

Act or React

"Those who love me, I will deliver; I will protect those who know my name. When they call to me, I will answer them; I will be with them in trouble, I will rescue them and honor them. With long life I will satisfy them, and show them my salvation" (Psalm 91:14-16).

Free will is one of God's greatest gifts to each and every one of us; or is it? Free will enables us to make our own choices, right or wrong, concerning our life and how we are going to live it. I honestly think I would freely have chosen to have no choices, had it been left up to me. I know God well enough to know that His choices far outreach my fondest dreams for my life. His choices afford me more love, peace, and happiness than I could ever choose on my own. I've found that most of the misery in my life has been as a direct result of my poor choices.

Anything that happens to us on a daily basis, or even a moment to moment basis, requires us to act or react to any particular given circumstance. That action or reaction is our choice to make. Whenever the phone rings with the most horrendous news beyond all our fears and imaginings, we can act or react. We can fall victim to circumstances and simply react to the evil befallen us. We can choose to act and take it to our God who makes countless promises such as the one in this Scripture. We are not left alone here to fend for ourselves in times of crisis, sickness, sin, evil, or any other thing that Satan can throw at us on any given day. God's wonderful living Word is full of promise after promise of how we should act and not react to this world we find ourselves in.

The simplest of actions is required of each Christian in our daily life.

We must make that freewill choice to act in the face of adversity. We can't simply sit and react to every plan gone awry around us. Even the paraplegic was required to act. He had spent years reacting to his infirmity, and Jesus gave one simple command, "Pick up your mat and walk." The man was required to make a choice. He could either continue to react to his circumstance, or he could act on Jesus' word and walk away a free man. Time after time, the Holy Bible gives us examples of people acting on God's promises. The Great Faker always takes just a twisted turn on the truth to wreak his wicked evil. I recently learned that the word "wicked" comes from the word "wicker." Evil is truth, but twisted like that wicker lawn furniture we see. If he can count on us to react instead of act, he's got us. He's got us in the grip of sin, disease, dread, and fear.

We can choose the action of leaning on God's promises. He promises to protect us. He promises to love us and answer us whenever we cry out to Him. He promises to be with us in times of trouble and lead us through the shadow of death. He promises each of us life abundant. He promises life everlasting. With all that promise, how can we not choose to act on His Word? Look back upon your life and recognize where you acted or reacted to any given situation. Without a doubt, you will see God's promise realized whenever you acted on His Word. Glory to God and His holy Word.

5

Attention Deficit Disorder

"He said, 'Go out and stand on the mountain before the LORD, for the LORD is about to pass by.' Now there was a great wind, so strong that it was splitting mountains and breaking rocks in pieces before the LORD, but the LORD was not in the wind; and after the wind an earthquake, but the LORD was not in the earthquake; and after the earthquake a fire, but the LORD was not in the fire; and after the fire a sound of sheer silence. When Elijah heard it, he wrapped his face in his mantle and went out and stood at the entrance of the cave. Then there came a voice to him that said, 'What are you doing here, Elijah'"(1Kings 19:11-13)?

"Be still, and know that I am God! I am exalted among the nations, I am exalted in the earth" (Psalms 46: 10).

My granddaughter is afflicted with a modern day diagnosis that is more prevalent with our youth and population than we would like to admit. She's not alone! There are more children today that are on drugs such as Ritalin than is healthy. I've recently even heard one adult confide that she has finally been diagnosed with ADD. She spent her whole life not knowing that she had this common neurological condition. Common though it may be, it is not an easy diagnosis to live with. Though medication is the answer for some individuals, it's out of the question for others.

One professional explained this disorder to me in layman's terms. If you were in the waiting room at the doctor's office, you would be hearing the phone ring, children chattering, low conversations of waiting room patients, and the office murmur of nurses and the like. When they called you back to the exam room, though the door shuts behind the nurse, you still are able to hear the hustle and bustle of the busy doctor's office. When that knock comes and doctor walks in, a healthy person's focus would then be directed toward the doctor and he would have all your attention. With ADD, the patient is unable to tune out all the other things going on. They continue to hear and be distracted by phone, nurses, patients, and office static while they are trying to zero in on the doctor. I could easily understand this scenario as being mind boggling.

I've discovered that once diagnosed by an audiologist, a person might be fitted with a device that is worn in the ear. This device is able to drown out all the underlying distractions that may be interfering with an ADD patient's ability to focus. I find this a viable alternative to taking drugs that have not been tested for long term effects on children.

This morning during my prayer time, my Divine Physician diagnosed me with ADD. I've been praying the prayer of Jabez for a while now, and am beginning to see results of earnest prayers. I'm currently reading a book on prayer and am seeking a more fulfilling prayer time each morning. In the book that I'm reading now the author relates a story about a missionary John Hyde (1865-1912). He became known as Praying Hyde. The story told of the long periods of silence that were throughout his prayers, and that peaked my interest. This morning's prayers for me would be filled with silence and listening time, no matter how long I had to wait.

Most Christians know what I'm speaking about when I share the following thoughts. We pray, praise, and lay down our burdens. We petition with all our requests and pleas. We do most of the talking. We seldom, if ever, give God the silence He requires of our spirits in order to speak to us about His will for our lives. I'm so guilty of not being still. It's so hard for me to be still. In the book of I Kings, Elijah didn't meet God in the wind, the earthquake, or the fire. He heard from our one true God in the sheer silence. The Bible tells us that Elijah was told to go to the mountain for the LORD was about to pass by. Though Elijah looked for him in the wind, the earthquake, and in the fire, he found Him, at last, in the sheer silence. In sheer silence God was able to make Himself known to Elijah. I fear God has passed by too many times in my life. Too many times, I fear I have not been still in order to really hear from Him.

As I tried to be still this morning, I heard birds chirping, traffic in the distance, planes flying overhead, neighbors mowing and on and on. Jesus let me know through my understanding of ADD that this had been part of the problem with my prayer life. Distractions are tools of Satan. We all owe it to ourselves to go off somewhere and be still in order to hear from God.

To know His will for our lives, we must be still and listen. We can recite all the right prayers, say all the proper words and still not have made a divine connection. I've spent times in prayer knowing that I've been in the holy presence of God. I've spent times in prayer that were simply punching the clock. Every Christian knows the difference. I am going to earnestly make an effort from this day forward to make that divine connection every time I go to Him in prayer.

Jesus is that ear device for every Christian to be able to focus. He can drown out all distractions going on around us. Satan flees from His presence. Call upon His name and be still. Be still and know God. Allow Him to take you to that secret place in your heart for the LORD is passing by today for each of us. We must not miss His passing!

6

Basking

"From His fullness we have all received grace upon grace" (John 1:16).

"I pray that you may have the power to comprehend, with all the saints, what is the breadth and length and height and depth, and to know the love of Christ that surpasses knowledge, so that you may be filled with all the fullness of God" (Ephesians 3:18-19).

Rainy, yucky, busy, and rushed are some thoughts that came to mind as I began my day. Much to do today; hope I feel better; hope the medicine kicks in quickly to enable me to get everything done. Go to the Lord and get that out of the way to begin the day.

My mind races through the motions and then, God reaches down and gives me a quick refresher course on grace. He is constantly using my cat, Boots of Grace (thus her name) to teach me the simplest of life lessons and the immensity of His grace. Repeatedly I've stated, "I'm a simple person and God speaks to me in simple ways."

As I hurriedly open my Bible, something behind me outside the window catches my attention. A bump, a distant cry; what was that? Thinking that the cats were still in the basement, I went to the door and to my surprise, there's Boots! Wet, crying, cold, and seeking comfort of home and hearth. I quickly get her in my lap with a fleece throw, drying and warming her. She's crying and writhing and basking in the comfort of the attention that she's now getting.

I'm reminded of a past lesson that God taught me about extremes.

Boots definitely, in five minutes, went from the extreme of chilling cold and wet weather, to the lap of warmth, comfort, and love. She was basking. No other word could describe her delight; yes, basking would be the word.

As I reflect on our past weekend away with the Lay Witness Mission, basking would have to be the word to describe the grace and fullness of God that abounded. We basked in fellowship with other believers; we basked in shared experiences. We basked in God's fullness, His love, and His grace. From prayers, to witnessing, to dining at the potluck suppers and coffees, we basked. God's grace and fullness was there to fill us beyond anything we could have hoped for.

God is so much bigger than we can imagine. He's alpha and omega, the beginning and the end. He's beyond our immediate awareness of Him. He's like the song says, out there in the distance, walking to the masses. He's all encompassing and His grace takes us from glory to glory. The anticipation and excitement grow in my spirit as I taste and bask in His grace. As He continues to lavish all His riches and glory into my life, I can't wait to see what's next.

Recently, learning about Porch Grace taught me that I'd been on that porch much too long. Like Boots, I was out there in the extreme of whatever might blow, but coming inside to God's fullness of grace has allowed me to bask and revel in the awesomeness of the God we serve. He's so much more than we could ever need or grasp hold of. Take Him out of the box today. Look for Him in the roads and byways of your life and recognize Him for Who He is. He is the One who loves you beyond measure, and is there just behind that door to let you in.

He'll take you inside to His comfort, mercy, love, and grace and have you purring like a kitten in no time. Allow Him to love you. Allow Him into your day. Allow Him to shower you with all that He has for you. Be open, be receptive, be found in Him, and bask, sweet child of God, bask. He's ready to surprise you today.

7

Bigger Than Pop

"…and they will see the Son of Man coming on the clouds of Heaven with power and great glory. And He will send out His angels with a loud trumpet call, and they will gather His elect from the four winds, from one end of heaven to the other" (Matthew 24:30-31).

As my granddaughter and I rode down the Interstate on the way to school this morning, the sun made a rather unusual display in the eastern sky. We both saw it at the same time. As the fog and clouds moved away from the sun, the figure-like array of light was breathtaking. I didn't voice my first thought, and in trying to share the moment with her, I said something to the effect that it looked much like fireworks or a huge fountain of water. Her next statement took my breath away.

"Nana, I think it looks like Jesus coming in the sky." That had also been my first thought, but I was hesitant to share with her for fear that she would not understand. I asked her to explain why she thought that it looked like Jesus. She quickly described the above scripture in the words of a nine-year-old child.

Somewhere and somehow, in her short nine year walk with God, she had fathomed an understanding of how Jesus would come again. She described that the sun would have lines of light shining down everywhere, and that everybody would be able to see it. I quickly thought of all the paintings and artwork that I had seen during my many years of walking with the Lord, and knew that was definitely man's vision of the second coming.

As we continued to revel in the solar and cloud display, our joy in seeing the figure of Jesus with hands outstretched from under a flowing white robe brought tears and smiles to both our faces. We talked about the fact that whenever Jesus does come to take us to heaven, we would be there together, and never fuss or squabble with each other again. We would be able to simply love and enjoy each other. We wouldn't have time-outs or punishments for misbehavior. We wouldn't have short tempers or bad days. We would have eternity together.

She then remarked that the sun was Jesus' head. She could see the light portraying Jesus on the cross. I could never see exactly what she was seeing, though I tried. I never saw the cross; I could only see the flowing white robe, with hands outstretched. I have no doubt that she could envision the cross in her mind.

As we continued our conversation, I said, " You know that God is not the sun, don't you? God is bigger than the sun." Then, I tried to explain that God was bigger than anything she could imagine. Her next statement summed it up, "You mean God is bigger than Pop?" I laughed when I told her that of course, God was bigger than Pop.

Later, coming home alone, I realized that she wasn't talking about bulk or size. She was talking about how big her Pop is in her life. No one or anything is bigger or more important to her than her Pop. Pop can work miracles. Pop can soothe hurts and Pop can bring her joy immeasurable. By telling her that God was bigger than Pop, I think I got my point across.

We should come to Him as little children. Yes, God is bigger than any Pop or person in our lives that we could possibly recall or name. He's real. He loves us beyond our deserving. He heals all our hurts. He fills us with joy and a zest for living that only He can. Yes, Jesus will come again in the clouds, as the Scriptures foretell, to take us away to God the Father; and what a glorious day that will be.

8

Boast in the Lord

"But God chose what is foolish in the world to shame the wise; God chose what is weak in the world to shame the strong. God chose what is low and despised in the world, things that are not, to reduce to nothing things that are, so that no one might boast in the presence of God. He is the source of your life in Christ Jesus, who became for us wisdom from God, and righteousness and sanctification and redemption, in order that, as it is written, 'Let the one who boasts, boast in the Lord'" (I Corinthians 1:27-31).

Recently, as someone shared his past and his dark side to me, he questioned that God would use him to help others. I'm reminded here that God used Peter, who denied Him and was a brash, and sometimes brutish, personality. God used King David, who was a mere back-country shepherd boy, who, after being chosen and anointed by God, fell into Satan's traps and committed adultery and, eventually, premeditated murder. God used Moses, a man with a speech impediment, who also was a murderer. God used the misguided and zealous Saul of Tarsus who, after meeting Jesus on the road to Damascus, was converted to become Paul. Paul's writings have as much, if not more, impact on the Gentiles and Christ's kingdom than anything we can read today.

In this Scripture from the letters to Corinth, Paul reminds us of his lowly estate and ours, in God's master plan. We are but vessels to be used so that His glory and His majesty might be reflected through us. The Bible tells us that "no one is good, no not one" (Romans 3:12). It also tells us that anything we might do that looks good is but filthy rags. Only by our merciful God working in and through us might we achieve anything worthwhile or purposeful. Indeed, when we are weak, He is strong!

As I spend time with God today, my eye catches the water reflection atop the blackish pool cover. The ladder, the trees, the clouds, and the beautiful Carolina blue sky are mirrored almost perfectly in the water that has pooled atop the dark cover. My first thought was of that picture of the lake out west somewhere that is crystal clear and reflects the mountains and beauty that lies beyond its banks. Then I thought of the muddy lakes around here that hardly reflect anything at all.

My simple mind grasps that the darker the background or bottom of the water, the clearer the reflection. We are called to be God's hands and feet here on earth. We are called to be children of God and a reflection of His love, mercy, and grace. It just may be that the darker our background, the more trials and struggles that we've come through, allows a clearer and more vivid reflection of God our Father. I know from my personal life, it makes it more than clear to me that anything worthwhile that I might do is His doing, not mine.

This Scripture tells us that God chose us for that very reason, that He might be glorified through us. He chose what was simple, foolish, weak, and despised by the world, so there would be no doubt from where the power source comes. It comes from Him. So if you doubt today that He can use you, rest your mind that He can. No matter what you've done, where you've been, He can turn all the hurt, the pain, the bad, and the ugly of your life into something beautiful where He might be reflected.

It's Him, not you or me; and He is more than able and glad to use our brokeness for His glory. Don't waste that painful past, allow Him access today to use even your life as He did Paul's life. Boast in Him and thank Him that the darker your background, the clearer His light and reflection might shine forth into a hurting and hurtful world. Praise Him and shine His reflection, child of God, shine His reflection.

9

Cat and Mouse

"Rejoice in the Lord always; again I will say, rejoice. Let your gentleness be known to everyone. The Lord is near. Do not worry about anything, but in everything by prayer and supplication with thanksgiving let your requests be made known to God. And the peace of God, which surpasses all understanding, will *GUARD* your hearts and your minds in Christ Jesus"(Philippians 4:4-7).

We've had a really unpleasant problem with Callie Cat (also known as "the killing machine"). By her natural genetic make up, she is a hunter and killer. We've jokingly said that if it moves, she kills it. We've cleaned up snakes, bunnies, birds, moles, field mice, and whatever else was the kill of the day. Although we amply feed her, she continues with her daily hunt. This week, she ferreted out some baby bunnies from the pompous grass near the pool. We were saddened after two of them drowned and she killed a third one. We were able to rescue the fourth baby bunny from the virtual jaws of death when we retrieved it from her tightly clenched teeth.

Anyone who has ever witnessed a cat and its prey knows that they don't simply kill their victims. They play, torment, and mutilate whatever is in their deadly snare. Someone told me yesterday that they had heard that cats drive their victim crazy with fear before they strike the fatal blow. I have seen her toy with moles and the like. As long as there is movement or signs of struggle, she will play "cat and mouse" with them. Once all the fight is out of her prey, she will casually walk off, losing all interest in it.

Satan toys with us much like a cat. He comes to rob, steal, and destroy.

He relishes in our struggles, worries, and fears. He causes just enough havoc in our lives to keep us agitated and preoccupied by fear. I think it was Joyce Meyer who defined fear as "False Evidence Appearing Real." Fear will drive the best of Christians insane and render them immobilized. When we are pre-occupied with fear, we are unable to function as productive and fruit-bearing Christians. This is why God has given us so many Scriptures like the one above as a weapon against Satan's "cat and mouse" game.

We must pray without ceasing. We must focus on God. We must not be distracted by the Devil's false evidence that appears to be real. His aim is to rob us of our joy and peace. God promises to guard us in all our ways. We must constantly remember Whose we are. The Devil is a danger to us, as long as we allow him the pleasures of playing with our minds. The Bible tells us that our mind is the Devil's playground. Like a cat, he enjoys the chaotic struggles we find ourselves in when we lose our peace. As long as we are aware that he is powerless to destroy us completely, we have a grasp on keeping our peace.

As Paul tells us in Philippians, we must REJOICE. It's virtually impossible to be fearful while you are rejoicing and praising and delighting in the Lord. This is a tool that God has given us to help us hold our peace. Rejoice in times of trial. Rejoice in sickness. Rejoice always. In all things rejoice, and enjoy the peace of Christ, which, indeed, surpasses all our understanding.

10

Caterpillars

"Blessed are those who hunger and thirst for righteousness, for they will be filled" (Matthew 5:6).

Boy, do I love to watch the butterflies! My granddaughter and I even planted three butterfly bushes in order to attract more of those lovely creatures. The day after we planted the bushes, we spent a whole afternoon catching black caterpillars off the pin oaks in the front yard. We would capture them and put them into a coffee can with lid. Those varmints were crawling everywhere on the trees, brick, and front porch. Ugh! I squashed a couple, then she squealed, "No Nana, I want them."

She loves any creepy, crawly thing. I felt sneaky when I gave her the coffee can with lid. I purposely didn't punch holes in the lid. I realize how devious I was. A seven-year-old didn't know that lack of oxygen would eventually be fatal. A forty-nine year old did realize that scientific fact, but didn't want to be a cruel Nana.

I felt a need to protect my trees from being eaten, but also wanted to appease my granddaughter's tender-heartedness. Needless to say, the next morning the caterpillars were dead. She took her news well; after all, she had enjoyed the previous afternoon playing with the black, horned varmints.

Today it hit me square between the eyes! No caterpillars, no butterflies! No varmints, no beautiful creatures. How could I have been so cruel and thoughtless? Aren't we all guilty of always wanting the end result without the preparation?

I cherish my relationship with God. He is a living, loving God. I'm at the stage in my life that I always dreamed of in my younger days. I do realize that I had to sacrifice to get to this place. Sacrifice may not be an appropriate word. Bible studies, disciple studies, Sunday School, building team, daily devotions, and time spent in prayer are not always convenient. Everyone has the same amount of time. There are twenty-four hours in each day.

There have been times that I felt I gave up something important in order to attend a class or read my Bible. How foolish I was! To make this point, I'll compare those preparations to the varmint caterpillars. I'm so very thankful to God that I didn't squash them or put them into a closed coffee can. Without those preparation times, I wouldn't be where I am in my relationship with God.

We can't have butterflies without caterpillars. It's a fact. God's gift of grace is free, but we do have a responsibility to be open and make ourselves available to His call. What a small sacrifice we are asked to make in order to receive the ultimate sacrifice. Find a caterpillar today and expect a beautiful butterfly to come your way.

11

The Children of God Are Safe

"...they offered Him gifts of gold, frankincense, and myrrh. And having been warned in a dream not to return to Herod, they left for their own country by another road" (Matthew 2:11).

Any parent knows the joy of those wonderful words, "The children are safe." I can remember numerous times of taking comfort from the fact that my children were safe in their beds. No matter what was going on in our lives at the time, just the knowledge that they were warm, fed, and safe from all harm was a blessing in itself. I knew where they were. I knew that that their needs were being met. I knew they were in no immediate danger. Comfort in these things brought me through many years of struggle raising three children.

As I awoke this morning my first thought was, "The children of God are safe." Where it came from, I don't know. I have no recollection of what I was dreaming or even thinking about in my sleep state. I simply know that thought is in the foremost part of my mind today. From past experiences, I've been awakened by a thought like this, gotten up, written whatever was on my mind, and later found out that it could have come only from God.

Reflecting on the life of Jesus this morning, I can see how God kept Him safe throughout His life on earth. Whenever there was no room in the inn for Jesus to draw His first human breath, God provided a warm cover from the elements. Though a lowly manger, God provided a place for the miracle to occur. When Herod plotted to kill the infant Jesus, God spoke to the wise men and Joseph in dreams. The wise men went home by another route, and Joseph fled to Egypt with Mary and baby Jesus. Again, when Jesus was left behind in a strange city, He was found safe in the temple going about His Father's business. Time after time, the Bible gives us examples of God keeping His own child safe and out of harm's way, at least until His appointed time had come.

God, through His abundant love for us, shows us the perfect example of a parent's love. He desires our safety as much as we desire it for our own children. As children of God, we can expect the same loving care that Jesus had during His life span before that fateful Passover in Jerusalem. God is true to His Word. The Bible says, "And because you are children, God has sent the Spirit of his Son into our hearts, crying, 'Abba! Father!' So you are no longer a slave but a child, and if a child then also an heir, through God"(Galatians 4:6,7).

Knowing fully well that I am a child of God, I can take comfort in the thought dancing through my mind today. "The children of God are safe." I can be reassured that no matter what I may face or have to encounter today, I'm safe. We all can be confident that no matter what we face in life, God has the solution for us. He's already worked it out, and we must but live it out, keeping Him at our center core.

Whenever you experience the holiness of this Christmastime, remember the holiness of your own personal Christmastime. As the angels sang and heralded the birth of Jesus the Son of God, they, too, sang at your own adoption into the family. We're all children of the one Living God and, indeed, safe.

(Just a footnote that within four months, God received my three grandchildren who were victims of a tragic car accident. I took comfort when I realized that He had let me know beforehand through a dream that they were indeed safe in His loving arms.)

12

Choose the Son

"For God so loved the world that He gave His only Son, so that everyone who believes in Him may not perish but may have eternal life"(John 3:16).

What is it about a cold, rainy day that puts us in the doldrums? It's just so much easier to fall prey to gloom and doom on a cloudy, rainy and gray day. Many a fabulous "pity party" has taken place on just such a day! The heavy, dark skies make a perfect backdrop motif for a good self-indulgent, "feel sorry for one's self" gala event. Sometimes the party might be justified. Sometimes the party is simply a way to shower ourselves with pampering that we feel we need.

Recently, my husband and I discussed this very subject. We ultimately decided that it was not the clouds, gray skies, nor rain that caused such melancholia, but more than likely it was the absence of the sun. It's a proven medical fact that the sun is conducive to our sense of well-being. There's even a medical condition called SAD that has been accredited to the absence of sunlight on the brain that eventually results in depression and anxiety. The bottom line is that simply, it's biologically, medically, and emotionally easier to be sad on a rainy day.

The recent accident that claimed the lives of my three granddaughters has caused me to soul search and rely heavily on my faith and personal relationship with God and His Son. Not once have I doubted His love, His control of the situation, and His ability to bring me through this valley. I know without a doubt that I'll come out of this tragedy a stronger servant and witness to my

LORD. I know without a doubt that He will be glorified by the recent events that devastated so many people. Good things have already happened. Children are planting trees, memorials are being planned, children have grieved and helped adults around them come to grips with grief. Three little girls who had such an effect of so many lives are now silent witnesses to God's love and mercy.

The Scripture above is such a familiar Scripture to all Christians. Many, who put no other Bible verse to memory, can recite this basic, faith scripture. I realize that I'm making a "play on words," that is an obvious one. How can a person possibly face life without the "Son?" As easy as it is to be miserable on a rainy day without the celestial sun, how much more astronomically impossible is it to face life without the Biblical Son of God? There are folks out in this world who live a life totally in those aforementioned cloudy, cold, and rainy surroundings. With this picture in my mind, I find it easier to show compassion and pity upon such people. They are in such a miserable existence without the Son of the Living God to support them and lead them through this journey of life that we all must walk through. We must pray for such people. Only God calls a person to Himself. We can pray that such persons might answer that call to accept Him.

I thank God that He gave His only Son, that I might have an abundant life everlasting. I praise God that His Son allows me access to His throne. I choose to live my life, by the grace and mercy of God, believing in that One Son who expels any cloudy, dark, or rainy thing that I could possibly face. Thank you Lord! On this BEAUTIFUL rainy day, I choose the Son! I choose not to wallow in self-pity or to be sad. I choose life and I choose happiness. I indeed choose the Son. Thank you for the Son, who can shine, on all my days, and through my life. Thank you for the Son who blesses anyone who might come into contact with those divine rays of light. Thank you, Lord, and all praise be given to You!

13

The Cross

"And Jesus came and said to them, 'All authority in heaven and on earth has been given to me. Go therefore and make disciples of all nations, baptizing them in the name of the Father and of the Son and of the Holy Spirit, and teaching them to obey everything that I have commanded you. And remember, I am with you always, to the end of the age'" (Matthew 28:18-20).

All through December, I was blessed with a sign of wonder, a star of light, as the Christmas carol sings of old. In the corner of my dining room floor, just as I go into the kitchen, the sunlight reflection of a perfect cross would appear. The phenomena happened around ten o'clock every morning in December that the sun shone. Of course, I know that the Christmas decorations adorning my front porch reflecting the sunlight had much in the physical realm to do with this sign of wonder, but God let me know that this cross blessed me more than I could ever comprehend.

The cross that appeared reassured me that my home, my life, and my ministry for Him were centered at the foot of the cross. All ground is equal at the foot of the cross. We're one in Christ at the foot of the cross. No man, woman, or child is loved more than another at the foot of the cross. We are equally loved, forgiven, and commissioned at the foot of the cross. The only differential thing at the foot of the cross is the willingness to receive and obey, and the conscious decision to follow wherever Christ might lead. He has promised to be with us in the valleys, as well as the mountaintops. He has commissioned us to go into the entire world, into all nations, into every heart.

We're not alone, and need not rely on our own understanding or our own qualifications. It's His kingdom, His power, and His light that we shine into this world. He's got it covered. He's shining that cross, which was such an ugly abomination to mankind into every believer's heart. His cross isn't something we can hang around our necks like a pendant. It's not something that we simply erect over a loved one's final resting place in the cemeteries. His cross should not simply adorn the buildings we erect to worship and praise His holy name. His cross was real. His cross was ugly, uncomfortable, and necessary.

The sign of the cross is something that every believer needs to embrace each and every day. Remember to remember what our Lord and Savior suffered and purified for our sakes. He did it! It is finished. He took that symbol of shame and suffering and made it into a new thing. He cleaned it, purified it, and offers it to each of us. Pick up your cross, the Bible tells us. We each have a cross to bear, and Jesus is carrying it with each of us, every day in every way. No matter the cross you suffer today, know that it's only a symbol of what He so willingly embraced because He loved us so very much.

Know that the cross you bear is but a means to an end. Know that whether the sun is shining to reflect the light of the cross on the mountaintops, or whether the clouds have rolled in and obscured the light that you so long for, the cross is there. The cross is real. The cross has sealed our fate for all eternity. The cross is a gift of God's grace to you and to me. The cross on which the Christ hung is the way, the truth, and the life.

James tells us, "My brothers and sisters, whenever you face trials of any kind, consider it nothing but joy, because you know that the testing of your faith produces endurance, and let endurance have its full effect, so that you may be mature and complete, lacking in nothing." (James 1:2-4).

Then the Bible says, "Therefore, since we are surrounded by so great a cloud of witnesses, let us also lay aside every weight and the sin that clings so closely, and let us run with perseverance the race that is set before us, looking to Jesus the pioneer and perfecter of our faith, who for the sake of the joy that was set before Him endured the cross, disregarding its shame, and has taken His seat at the right hand of the throne of God" (Hebrews 12:1-2).

Remember, all authority was given Him in heaven and on earth, this Scriptures tell us. Be a "kingdom dweller" here, now, and for all eternity. We pray His kingdom come, His will be done on earth as it is in heaven, in the Lord's Prayer. His kingdom is not something far off in eternity. His kingdom is here, now, today, and He hung on that cross so that you might have an abundant life, and be a kingdom dweller for all eternity, beginning this moment now. So pick up your cross, no matter how uncomfortable or ugly, count your blessings, and glean whatever you must to persevere and become the disciple that He's called you to be. We're not alone; He's with each of us, until the end of the age. The Bible tells us so.

14

Day by Day

"So we do not lose heart. Even though our outer nature is wasting away, our inner nature is being renewed day by day. For this slight momentary affliction is preparing us for an eternal weight of glory beyond all measure, because we look not at what can be seen but at what cannot be seen; for what can be seen is temporary, but what cannot be seen is eternal" (2 Corinthians 4:16-17).

"We can't look off into the future; we just have to take it day by day," my old school friend just advised me on the phone. God has put an old friend back into my life after years of absence. I know that God is a connector of people, and today I think that I might see His guidance and plan for our renewed friendship. She's helped me so much in the past couple of years, to face unfathomable tragedy and heartache. Without realizing it, she's helped me today face an eternal reality that's been hiding just behind my temporal view.

This friend had a challenged child the same age as my oldest child. My daughter would come home from school talking about some of the challenges that her son faced. My tenderhearted daughter always seemed to take a personal interest in her school friend, despite his handicaps. Children can be so cruel to another child that isn't quite up to par. My friend tells me today that she could write a book on the heartaches of raising such a child. From birth he had been a life trial for my friend, and now, in hindsight, I can see how special a person she really is. God chose her to raise His, not her, child of affliction.

I realize that the above Scripture is talking about our diseased bodies wasting away before our impending death. Yet, today it says a little more to me.

It speaks not only of an acute or chronic medical condition, but could also apply to a congenital birth defect. A challenged child could face a lifetime of affliction. The key here is to realize that this life is indeed temporal. The future for a child such as this is eternal bliss. The future when this life is over will hold rewards of its own. Only God knows why He creates physically or mentally challenged children. Perhaps He does it to allow those around the child to mature into the people they need to become.

The Bible tells us that He knows us even before we are knit in our mother's wombs; therefore, God does know what a child will face, long before that child comes into this world. A loving God will equip and protect that child that is, not less of a person, but actually more of a person, because they don't fit into the mold from which the majority of us were cast.

That child, more often than not, is more loving, more forgiving, and most likely oblivious to much of the hurt and ridicule going on around them. That child keeps us so close to God. That child wears on our nerves and convicts us of our impatience and shortcomings. Simple things like homework become so stressful. And yet, that child, who at one moment has us in stroke-mode, the next moment, may be stroking our very heartstrings. That child is the most precious of all persons in our lives because God chose that child to be as special as they surely are.

As we shared our experiences this morning, I listened to my own advice to her. Instead of being burdened by raising such a child with ongoing challenges, we are blessed to be a part of God's plan for that special child. Education and day to day life, with all its struggles, seem multiplied with such a child, and yet, if we can but take it day by day, God's Word says we might be renewed.

As I think about the future for the special child in my life, I must not choose to worry about unseen dangers. I must choose to take it day by day and not lose heart. This Scripture takes on a whole new meaning in my spiritual journey. God's Word tells us that He puts before us life and death. He entreats us to choose life. God allows us to choose. I choose from this day forward to take it day by day, and trust in Him, and lean not on my own understanding.

15

Don't Pack it All Away

"When the angels had left them and gone into heaven, the shepherds said to one another, 'Let us go now to Bethlehem and see this thing that has taken place, which the Lord has made known to us.' So they went with haste and found Mary and Joseph, and the child lying in the manger. When they saw this, they made known what had been told them about this child; and all who heard it were amazed at what the shepherds told them. But Mary treasured all these words and pondered them in her heart. The shepherds returned, glorifying and praising God for all they had heard and seen, as it had been told them" (Luke 2:15-20).

As I prepare to pack away all the beautiful trimmings and decorations of this past Christmas, I am somewhat saddened. It's this way every year. I drag my feet and don't really get into the spirit of clearing away all the bright reds, gold, and vivid colors of Christmas. For an all too short time, my home dances with colors. I trim each nook and cranny. Decking the halls of my home with Christmas always brings me joys and satisfactions like no other time of the year. Whether trimming each window, putting a bright red bow here or there, or simply placing symbols of the season in a bathroom or forgotten corner of my home, I enjoy the glitter and glamour of Christmas. I know all too well how drab and neutral my home becomes after all these festive colors and reminders of the holiday are packed away into boxes for next year.

Each year as I age, Christmas seems to come and go faster and faster. I learned long ago that the preparation and decorating times prior to the holiday

33

are to be savored and enjoyed. The holiday in reality is a season of love, not just one day to be crammed full of gift opening and feasting; and then plop, it's over! I fear that's where so many folks lose the full importance of Christmas. We're celebrating the birthday of our Lord and Savior, but Christmas also is the celebration of family, life, and goodwill toward our fellow man. These things are bright and cheerful and bring us happiness, like the colored lights, the tinsel, and the decorations that we lavish everywhere during the season.

That holiest of nights, when the baby Jesus was born, the angels sang, heralded His birth, and appeared among the shepherds on that lonely hillside near Bethlehem, was a spectacular night! Wow! Can you possibly picture the glorious colors, tinsel-like flashes of heavenly light, or the sounds of angelic singing? Those shepherds were richly blessed with all the divine colors and decorations that heaven could bestow upon the earth. What a glorious gift God gave us that night! His angels decked the halls of heaven with such glory that it spilled down onto the darkened night and the shepherds who were keeping watch over their flocks. When the angels left, the Bible tells us that the shepherds went in haste to find the Child. They shared their divine experience and amazed even those who had witnessed the actual birth of the Christ Child. The Bible continues to tell us that Mary treasured these things in her heart and that the shepherds went away glorifying and praising God.

As I box away my Christmas decorations this year, I'm going to treasure these things in my heart. I'm not going to pack it all away! I'm going to thank God for the love shared with my family. I'm going to glorify God for the moments spent with those dearest to me. I'm going to praise God for the laughter, the joys, and those precious moments that He so graciously allowed us to have this Christmas season. I'm going to rush with haste to the Christ Child, and glorify and praise Him for all that He so mercifully gives me. Don't pack it all away this year. Keep that true meaning of Christmas treasured in your heart! Be as those first shepherds were after all the glitter and glamour was over; go with haste, glorifying and praising His holy name. Amaze the world!

16

Don't Smell Like Smoke

"...and the satraps, the prefects, the governors, and the king's counselors gathered together and saw that the fire had not any power over the bodies of those men; the hair of their heads was not singed, their tunics were not harmed, and not even the smell of fire came from them" (Daniel 3:24-27).

To be put into a fiery furnace like Shadrach, Meshach, and Abednego, seems to me to be the ultimate persecution for a Christian to endure. I know that crucifixion was ranked as the cruelest death in biblical times, yet, to be burned alive is abhorrent to me.

These three men exhibited a faith beyond anything that a modern Christian may ever be asked to exhibit. Or did they? As Christians, we are all asked to enter a hypothetical fiery furnace each and every day. Once we've made the ultimate choice and commitment to accept and follow Jesus, we are asked to make a daily choice. We must choose life!

Each day the Evil One can come into our lives and weigh us down with sin, anxiety, worry, sickness, disease and all kinds of negative things. We are in a position each day to choose life and live it abundantly, or we can give in to all the negativity around us and be burned alive. We can focus on that fourth man in the fire and not be harmed.

I know lots of Christians that are strong in their faith and have come through the fires unscorched. I know only a few Christians who came through not even smelling like smoke. These Christian's positive attitudes have even taken away that scorched smell from their tunics.

I think as Christians, it's our duty to make that choice each day, to focus not on the difficulties around us, but to focus on the God who will help us through those difficulties. We must not complain or indulge in self-pity. When the unchurched look at us, going through life's trials and fires, they need to be puzzled by our positive attitudes. They need to ponder as to why or what we have to be so joyous and happy about. When they look at our individual difficulties and circumstances, and see how God leads us through them, they will desire to know that God who can do such a thing. They will desire to have what we have. By focusing on that fourth man in the fiery furnace, who is Jesus along side us, we too can not even smell like smoke.

17

Extreme Joy

"Very truly, I tell you, you will weep and mourn, but the world will rejoice; you will have pain, but your pain will turn into joy…On that day you will ask nothing of me. Very truly, I tell you, if you ask anything of the Father in my name, He will give it to you. Until now you have not asked for anything in my name. Ask and you will receive, so that your joy may be complete" (John 16:20, 23-24).

I love extremes. It has long been one of my favorite things. I love to throw open the French doors on a damp and gloomy day like this, and read in the comfort of my recliner with a nice, warm throw, keeping my feet and legs cozy. Years ago, I remember writing a short story about the joy that waking up on a chilly morning brought, whenever I could shuffle the covers around and expose my foot to the raw cold, only to bring it back under the toasty warmth of covers. A simply joy, true, but a joy for me, nonetheless.

A chill that is pushed away by a blazing fire is another extreme that brings comfort and enjoyment to mind. I've often, since childhood, enjoyed the extreme of sitting by an open window during a rain shower, just to enjoy the dry protection and warmth just inside the window. Extremes make us appreciate the joys of comfort and lack of discomfort. Extremes make us feel alive and animated in this life that our spirits journey through, to the eternal life that awaits each of us. Eternity is our goal, and this journey called life is but an experience of physical extremes.

If we didn't travel through valleys, we wouldn't appreciate the mountaintop joys of this journey. If we were never sick and in physical pain, we'd never know the full joy of a pain-free and healthy day. Had we not lost loved ones or mourned the passing of them, how would we be able to imagine the fullness of joy that loving that person brought into our journey through this life? If it weren't for the bad times, how could we thank God for the good times and blessings that He so richly rains into our lives? God is a God of extremes!

Had we not had our hearts broken from time to time, would we really see and appreciate the healing process, as God heals those broken hearts to make us stronger? The Bible is full of extreme examples. Some that come to mind are the first shall be last; in death there is life; in giving we receive...on and on, the Bible teaches us that God's kingdom is full of extremes that are upside down to our way of thinking in this realm.

The above Scripture jumps out at me as I read it this morning. How in the world can pain turn into joy? Pain is something we all will experience in one way or another during our journey through the extremes of this life. Pain doesn't equate to a joyful experience in my way of thinking...but there again, God's thoughts are not our thoughts, and His ways are far higher than our ways, the Bible tells us. So it's reasonable to think that our extreme God has a plan for all our pain. His plan is to turn it into joy in its fullness.

Fullness of joy can only be realized when we allow our extreme God to work in our lives. We must allow Him to work all things in our lives for good. We must believe and trust that He is able to turn all our pain into something beneficial to our lives. As The Bible tells us, "You have turned my mourning into dancing; You have taken off my sackcloth and clothed me with joy" (Proverbs 30:11). Fullness of joy is a divine extreme, made possible through God's mercy and grace that is available to each of us.

Believe what His Word promises. Meditate upon His holy Word, and ask in the name above all names. Then, open your hearts to receive! Receive all that He has for you that will come from all the pain and brokeness that you will experience, so that your joy may be complete. Further on in The Bible, John tells us, "…I speak these things in the world so that they may have my joy made complete in themselves" (John17:13). It's His joy; it's real and attainable, or Jesus would not have said it. Receive it today, and experience that extreme and complete joy that is yours through life with Jesus the Son of the living God.

18

Eye of the Needle

"...it is easier for a camel to go through the eye of a needle than for someone who is rich to enter the kingdom of God..." (Matthew 19:16–30).

Anyone who has been blessed to visit the holy lands has seen first hand, the Biblical "eye of the needle." In Jerusalem we saw the smaller gates within the huge ancient gates. Our guide explained that this gate within a gate was called the needle's eye gate. After nightfall, if anyone wanted to enter the city, they would have to unload their camel, and have the enormous animal lie on its stomach and crawl through this smaller entry gate. This was a safety feature against having an army of men storming through the larger gate, had it been opened in the darkened night.

This ancient precaution was an eye opener for me. Having read this particular Scripture passage, I had long ago come to the conclusion that it would be virtually impossible for a rich man to enter the kingdom, since I had visualized a camel literally trying to go through a sewing needle's eye. After the guide explained that indeed it was possible for a camel to go through the eye of a needle, my whole thinking changed.

I can see how a rich man can, indeed, enter the kingdom with some effort on his part. He must lay down his burden or riches. He must remove his riches from his person, and enter only as the unencumbered person that God created. Worldly titles or wealth does not impress God. As the camel laden with goods and equipment strapped to his back cannot enter through the needle gate, neither can the rich man come into the kingdom with anything other than

God's grace and a living relationship with God the Father. In essence, when a rich man comes to that point in his thinking, he indeed is no longer a wealthy man, but merely a lowly servant of God. He has traded his earthly riches for something far greater.

Riches are not burdensome things. It's how a man views or values his riches; that is the important thing. Those riches must never separate a man from God. A man's relationship with God is by far more valuable than any earthly gold. God doesn't desire that we all be poor. God's desire is that we love Him above all things. In God's kingdom, a rich man is the same as a poor man. We are all one in Christ. It just may be that the rich man has to go through a little more effort to enter that gate than the poor man does. God, help us to remember that it's only through grace that any of us may enter Your kingdom.

19

Fertile Soil

"That same day Jesus went out of the house and sat beside the sea. Such great crowds gathered around Him that He got into a boat and sat there, while the whole crowd stood on the beach. And He told them many things in parables, saying, 'Listen! A sower went out to sow. And as he sowed, some seeds fell on the path, and the birds came and ate them up. Other seeds fell on rocky ground, where they did not have much soil, and they sprang up quickly, since they had no depth of soil. But when the sun rose, they were scorched; and since they had no root, they withered away. Other seeds fell among thorns, and the thorns grew up and choked them. Other seeds fell on good soil and brought forth grain, some a hundredfold, some sixty, some thirty. Let anyone with ears listen'" (Matthew 13:1-9)!

This familiar parable has taken on many different depths in my Christian walk. I would venture to say the meaning directly reflected the condition of my soil. I can quickly relate to the path where the seed/Word was sown, and I simply didn't have the capacity or the God given knowledge to receive it and apply it into my life.

It's easy to remember times in my life where my rocky and thin soil bed didn't allow much of a root system for the seed to grow. Though I knew that it sounded like the truth and good news, it didn't take much for me to forget my religion and revert back into my sinful nature.

I also remember my thorny years, when those around me refused to join me or encourage my growth in a relationship with God. Whenever God creates a new creature in us, sometimes we must leave behind not only a lifestyle, but also certain people in our lives. We have a new and right spirit in us that no longer wants to continue the common bond of sin that we previously enjoyed with those people.

I truthfully believe that I'm now enjoying my fertile soil years. My soil has been turned, fertilized, and sown. I can remember many years ago praying to be fertile soil. Had I known the price of that rich soil that allows roots to grow deep into our spirit, I would have possibly been a little more hesitant about the prayer request. I know beyond a doubt that I would pay the price over and over to be in the high-end real estate of life.

Think about it practically! The cheaper the price is of the land, the cheaper the quality. You can easily purchase something, in a run down and poor section of town, without much effort or discomfort. The real estate value reflects the quality of the land. Land and soil are synonymous words.

Look around you at those who have faced horrendous trials in life, and see how God is able to use their testimonies to His glory. The richness of the soil embellishes the quality of the witness. Fertile soil is expensive. It must be tilled, turned, fertilized, and watered constantly. There is a labor factor that figures into fertile soil also.

That expensive price was paid for all of us on Calvary. Jesus paid the ultimate price as the true suffering servant. We merely partake of His life and we are recipients of that fertile soil. Yes, life will bring us many trials and tribulations that turn and plow our soil, but we can rest in the fact that as long as we are in Christ, all of that turbulence and testing is for our good. We can grow and be richer for the experiences. Our soil becomes more fertile with each chop of the hoe or furrow of the plow.

20

Fill Your Bag

"He who descended is the same one who ascended far above all the heavens, so that He might fill all things" (Ephesians 4:1).

Yesterday's children's sermon by a local author consisted of brown paper bags. He shared with the children that their lives were like these brown paper bags. We have a choice to fill them with good things, bad things, nothing at all, or simply crumple them and throw them away. This visual demonstration was an eye opener for some.

When my four-year-old grandson recently made a simple request, I initially thought it was cute. After spending the night, he got through with breakfast and said, "Nana, let's go watch Joyce Meyer or Judge Judy on TV." I laughed at this statement coming from such a small fellow. He was ready to be filled. Being young, he was open to whatever I chose to fill him with for the day. That's a big responsibility that we all need to take seriously.

"Why in the world would you want to watch either program? Where did you learn about them?" was my next question. He relayed that I watched Joyce Meyer and his other grandmother always watched Judge Judy in the mornings. This drove home the fact that little eyes are always watching us even when we don't realize it. They can see what we are filling our lives with more than we can.

His request has bothered me at intervals in the past week, and when I heard the children's sermon, I knew why. We are all filling our bags/lives with something. Whenever we put good stuff in, we can expect good stuff to come out. If we fill our bags with garbage and bad things, how can we expect things to go along joyously and smoothly?

God gave us His inspired Word in the Bible to fill our spirits with every possible good thing to live our lives. We find every excuse not to go to the source of our joy and simply immerse ourselves in this soul feast. I'm amazed at the folks who are sweet Christian people that never find the time to read their Bibles. If an occasional dose of God's Word gives us joy, why then wouldn't we want to get as much as we possibly could?

I'm guilty of struggling too long with problems or things before taking it to God. I now am finding myself turning to His Word more quickly in order to get things in my life back on track. God has shown me over and over that if I fill my bag/life with good things about Him, I'm stronger and more at peace. Like those hard-hearted and stubborn Israelites, I find myself continually trying to do things on my own. Will we never learn?

Life is hard, stressful, busy, and spinning out of control for most of us. It's out of our control, but not out of God's control. He gave us Jesus Christ to fill ourselves, in order to live this life abundantly. It's too easy! We need only be filled. Empty us of self, and be filled. This Bible verse tells us that He came so that He might fill all things. To be filled with Christ is the life abundant of which the Bible speaks. Fill your bag with good things. Fill your bag with encouragement, joy, and peace. Fill your bag with the good news. Jesus came that we may be filled with His glory. It's our choice!

21

Fragrance

"But thanks be to God, who in Christ always leads us in triumphal procession, and through us spreads in every place the fragrance that comes from knowing Him. For we are the aroma of Christ to God among those who are being saved and among those who are perishing; to the one a fragrance from death to death, to the other a fragrance from life to life. Who is sufficient for these things? For we are not peddlers of God's word like so many, but in Christ we speak as persons of sincerity, as persons sent from God and standing in His presence" (II Corinthians 2:14-17).

Fragrance is a beautiful word to describe a pleasing and beautiful smell. When we think of the word fragrance, automatically something lovely like a flower, or pleasant like a perfume comes to mind. Aroma on the other hand usually makes one think of food. Food definitely has aroma that arouses our senses like no other smell we can internalize does. Smell is a word that can go either way; it can smell really, really good or it can just plain smell, causing our noses to crinkle up and turn away in a repulsive and evasive motion.

I find it interesting that the above Scripture gives us a full meaning of that word fragrance. That inference of "from death to death" has to be a smelly situation. We, as Christians, are to strive for that aroma and fragrance that would attract the lost and the least to our precious Lord and Savior, Jesus, the very essence of this life and our eternal life. Without Him, none of us would ever be judged righteous enough to live in the hereafter. But for Him and God's mercy and grace, we would all be perishing without hope.

Our pastor spoke about the smell of Jesus in her sermon last week. Are we as Christians witnessing about His saving grace and His power in our lives? Are we being living testimonies of His righteousness and love for all? Do we have the fragrance of knowing Him and sharing Him with others, or are we simply that smelly situation that makes others' noses crinkle up and be repulsed?

I picked a camellia yesterday to give to the pastor. It was absolutely pristine in appearance. Each petal and leaf that I picked from the stem was perfect and not flawed in any way. The color was vibrant and pleasing to the eye. As I brought it to my nose to inhale what had to be a fragrance unrivaled in springtime, I was shocked to find there was no smell at all. Immediately God brought to mind, "This is a Christian without the smell of Jesus upon him."

Are we pew potatoes who simply sit and look the part of a good Christian? Do we look, feel, speak, and act like a good Christian, doing what we think is all the right things? Or, are we out in the world, the streets, and the byways smelling like Christ had to smell as he reached out and touched the leper? As He knelt and washed the disciples' feet, he had the fragrance of God upon Him. As He hung upon that wretched cross with His body beaten and marred beyond all recognition, I envision the matted hair, the clotted blood, and the dripping sweat a sweet fragrance of God's eternal and everlasting love for each one of us.

We are all called to be that fragrance of God that will call all of His children home. All His children are every color, creed, and race. The New Testament tells us, "…and live in love, as Christ loved us and gave Himself up for us, a fragrant offering and sacrifice to God" (Ephesians 5:2). My prayer today is that we Christians are a fragrance of God to the hurting world, and not that repulsive smell that will drive them away from His eternal saving grace. That fragrance acceptable to God is always pleasing in His sight, and you may find it today. Go down upon your knees into His presence and receive His love, His forgiveness, His mercy, and His grace; and yes, His fragrance will linger.

22

The Garden

(Genesis 2, 3).

Have you ever wondered why Satan was allowed into the Garden of Eden? Why would God allow this tempter into an otherwise perfect paradise? Sure, Satan had been cast down from heaven, but it seems to me that God should have somehow kept this great deceiver from access to Adam and Eve. Why was the tree of the knowledge of good and evil planted in the midst of the garden? Why was temptation ever introduced as an option in this perfect Garden of Eden?

My fenced back garden/pool area is a virtual and real example to me of the Garden of Eden. The birds have fed there safely without a hint of danger. Bunnies have nestled beneath the deck to live free from harm. Neighborhood dogs are not a threat to any creature that gains access into this guarded haven. Though noises outside of traffic, barking, trains, and the like sound menacing, there is no threat of danger inside these highly fenced walls of safety.

Recently, a dangerous threat was introduced into this otherwise Mecca of tranquility. A stray kitten was rescued from starvation atop a tree out front. Having been there for an undetermined amount of time, she was weak, scraggly, and frightened. We've fed her abundantly and offered her the safety of our back garden fenced area. She seems to have welcomed these garden walls as a safe harbor from all that the world must have hit her with during her ordeal. Not having a clue as to where she came from or why she was up our tree, our family has accepted her as a member of our household.

This morning as I watch her lounge and bathe in the sun, I'm made aware of a harsh reality. When the wren came to the feeder, she assumed an attack position and lunged. She's small and not an adept hunter as of yet. This morning was a practice drill. She's practicing her hunting skills like any cat. They are genetically programmed to do this. I cannot discourage her from something that is her natural trait and in her genetic makeup. The wren flew to a nearby crepe myrtle bush in utter surprise. As many other birds, he had grown accustomed to the feeder and its aforementioned safety. My fear is that the birds will no longer frequent the feeder that I've so enjoyed watching them use.

As I watch Callie Cat playfully chase her ball, I'm struck by the fact that this playful, mischievous kitten can and will be a life threatening menace to the life style of my version of a modern day Garden of Eden. This kitten will have to make a choice one day. She can continue to trust that I will daily feed and water her and give her all that she needs to sustain life, or, she can follow her natural inclination to hurt and kill a bird for food that she doesn't really need.

This revelation also answers my original questions. We as human beings can trust God with our whole hearts to answer all our needs, or we can make a choice to follow our sinful natures. Once Adam and Eve tasted from the tree of knowledge, they lost their innocent and trusting relationship with God. God has from the beginning offered us a choice. This choice is His gift of free will. Our only defense or hope from the effects of Adam's choice is the choice that Jesus the Christ offers each of us.

We can choose life in Christ and overcome the death sentence that Adam chose for all mankind. His choice created a gap of separation from the living God that he had trusted. Through Christ we can overcome our sinful natures. It may be our natural and genetic makeup to be sinful creatures yet God gave us Jesus to overcome them. Through the cross of Jesus, we can bridge that gap. We can again have fellowship with the one true God. It's all about relationship! Our entire life is nothing without our living relationship with God the Father.

23

Genuine Love

"Let love be genuine; hate what is evil, hold fast to what is good; love one another with mutual affection; outdo one another in showing honor. Do not lag in zeal, be ardent in spirit, serve the Lord. Rejoice in hope, be patient in suffering, persevere in prayer. Contribute to the needs of the saint; extend hospitality to strangers" (Romans 12:9-13).

In Philippians 2:12, Paul tells us to work out our own salvation with fear and trembling. While on the Potter's wheel today, He definitely is dealing with me concerning "genuine love." I remember asking a pastor many years ago as to why it was so much easier for me to love strangers and show compassion to those whom I hardly knew than it was to continue showing compassion or loving those closest to me. We all have family members that we find harder to love than others. We all have close relationships that seem never to come up to our expectations of what we think they should be. I'm speaking of that family member or close friend who continues to abuse your love toward them. No matter how hard or how long you extend the hand of help or love, they repeatedly "bite the hand that feeds them," to coin an old phrase.

When my husband and I first moved to this small town many years ago, we met a colorful character that was from Cuba. He could not for the life of him pronounce the word genuine. He would always leave off the 'g' and say, "enuine." We bought some "enuine" pool furniture from him and used to chuckle and fondly poke fun at what an "enuine," sweet person he was. I admit to wondering why he would use a word so readily that he apparently could not pronounce. He did love to use enuine, though, in nearly every other sentence.

Christians use the word love to describe everything from God to his or her favorite hobby. We flaunt the word as if Christians have a patent on it. After all, our God is a God of love. We must share with the world His love. I'm always unnerved when I go out to eat after church and see other Christians at the buffet bar completely unable to show "love or hospitality" to strangers with so little a thing as a smile or hello. I know they just came from church, not from their "love walk," because they are dressed in their Sunday best. I'm sinfully too proud of myself that I'm able to show hospitality and love to strangers, sometimes to the embarrassment of my husband. I love people is my all too often used comment.

The Potter tells me this morning that just maybe I'm like that man who couldn't pronounce genuine. Is the love I feel for people genuine? If so, why do I find it so hard to love those that I know so well? Love can come in many different forms. Love can be blind, possessive, self-serving, and not the agape, unadulterated and genuine love that our God pours out on us so mercifully. We don't deserve it; we almost daily "bite the hand that feeds us" that genuine love that we strive to attain in our hearts. I've often heard it said, "You can't give away what you don't have." We can only receive genuine love from Father God. Once we receive it into our hearts, we then can genuinely love ourselves and therefore pass it on to others. Lord, give me wisdom and truth in my inward being to know genuine love that I might in turn pass it on to others.

Genuine love loves those we meet along the way and may never see again. Genuine love is unselfish, undemanding, and not willful. Genuine love does not bind, hinder, or have any expectations from the recipient. It balances and harmonizes. Genuine love is from God and does not give up on us, no matter how much we mess up or reject it. Genuine love forgives, forgets, and loves beyond any shortcoming or sin. Remember that He loved us when we were yet sinners; therefore, we must genuinely love, no matter the circumstance.

Thank you, Father God, for loving me when I was far from You in sin and continuing to love me as I draw closer to You and become that errant family member that is so very hard to love. Seeing myself as that hard to love person gives me a better understanding of genuine love. I praise You and genuinely love You with my whole heart as I, with fear and trembling, continue to work out my salvation. Glory to Father God and His Son Jesus for being the genuine example of perfect love.

24

Glory Days

"...I desire that you insist on these things, so that those who have come to believe in God may be careful to devote themselves to good works; these things are excellent and profitable to everyone" (Titus 3:8).

As I finish up my devotion today, a still small voice inside brings to mind the book of Titus. It's nowhere near the Scripture I have just finished, and to be honest, I had to search page by page to locate its hiding place in the New Testament. For further use, I've logged it in my brain as the little book just before Hebrews. Since it contains only three chapters, I decide that the small voice made it sound important enough to warrant an entire reading.

Paul is speaking to his brother in Christ, Titus, who was left behind in Crete to help set up the early church. As I get to the last two chapters, the message that God wanted me to glean today jumped out at me. Good works are always a touchy subject with me. I'm prone to trying to do good works to the point that sometimes I feel guilty about my intentions or what others may think of me. I'm not trying to earn anything; I'm simply trying to pay back and do the things that God puts on my heart to do. I must admit that at times, I spread myself thinner than I would care to admit. I also admit that sometimes the inability to say no gets me into ventures that may not be entirely ordained by God.

From the above Scripture, God reassures me that my heart is in the right place and my eagerness to solve the world's problems comes from my devotion to Him. My heart is for everyone to know the love and grace that is so readily available to all of us. If God can use me in any way to help someone come to know Him better, I'm a willing servant. Those are my personal glory days.

I've tasted the sweet joy numerous times in my life. I feel so blessed when someone's words, hug, or even a simple smile lets me know that I've made a difference in his or her day. No matter how small the gesture I've made, to know that I've touched them with the hand of God empowers me as a Child of God. It's again what I'll refer to as my glory days.

I've held a precious child in a foreign land that had no idea what I was saying when I told her that "Jesus loved her and so did I." I've felt her little arms enfold me and kiss my wet cheek as we had to say goodbye forever. I've made friends in foreign lands that are forever in my thoughts, prayers, and heart. Though I may never see them again this side of Heaven, I know that through God's divine plan, we will spend all eternity together.

I've sung "Because He Lives" with a man in an unknown tongue as we exited an elevator in Galilee. Our only communication in a common language was "Jesus Christ is my life." Numerous times in my everyday life, I've connected with a friend, acquaintance and, at times, a stranger, and shared the love of Christ. Rich man, poor man, any man found in the light of the Love of God knows that joyous, warm, reassurance that we are not alone in this World. Those are indeed my glory days.

As I finish my daily devotion with prayer, my thoughts are with my friend in Dominica, and another friend in Bolivia. I've been on those building teams and know that God blesses the participants far more than the recipients. I've felt His Mighty Hand as He uses a team of servants ready to be His hands to help a hurting world. I feel, not a little, but a lot envious of my brothers in Christ who are in the middle of God's Will at this very moment. As Henry Blackaby says, "God is ALWAYS at work around us. We simply need to have the eyes to see Him at work and join Him where He is."

We can all have glory days by simply allowing Christ to love the world through us. A willing servant knows that His love must be shared. It must not stay in the servant, but be poured out into the lives of everyone we come in contact with during our each and every day. In these quiet times when I'm not involved of God's divine global works, I can be content knowing that something as simple as a hug, as my granddaughter gets off the school bus today, can be just as much a glory day.

25

The God of Restoration

"Do not remember the former things, or consider the things of old. I am about to do a new thing" (Isaiah 43:18-19).

"The days are surely coming, says the LORD, when I will make a new covenant with the house of Israel...I will put my law within them...for I will forgive their iniquity, and remember their sin no more" (Jeremiah 31:31-34).

"And the One who was seated on the throne said, 'See, I am making all things new.' Also He said, 'Write this, for these words are trust-worthy and true.'" (Revelation 21:5).

Springtime is such a visual example of God's grace and blessing of restoration. The barren trees that had given up their foliage and braved the cold, wintry onslaught are now decked out with glorious blooms and buds of promise. Hard and recently frozen flowerbeds are adorned with new growth popping through the mulch. Daffodils are blooming. Brilliantly colored crocus show their presence amidst drab browns and grays. The dead stubble of lawns is now coming alive with the dark vibrant greens that will soon demand our weekly attention. Spring, above all seasons, sings and shouts of God's restoration.

Once upon a time, a man named Adam walked in the cool of the morning. He walked in the Garden of Eden with the God, who created him. He walked and talked and communed with the Creator. God openly gave him his heart's desires. He created many things for the man's enjoyment and pleasure. God's love for the man was apparent in that He was in continual relationship with the man, Adam. God's love and grace were sufficient to make the man happy. The man lived in truth and light.

Something evil came along and lured the man, Adam, away from his Utopian life. Man fell from grace. God's love and grace were still sufficient but man chose another path. Many years and generations were lived out in unrest and separation from the Creator. Hard, cold, and wintry years of darkness ensued. But the God of restoration brought things around in full circle. The Creator never gave up on man. He created the second Adam called Jesus the Christ. The new covenant would restore man to his original relationship with God the Creator. God would forgive mans' iniquities and sins. Man could again live in truth and light.

Spring not only brings restoration to all of nature; it also brings us the Easter story. Springtime brings us the story of the second Adam. He was sent by the Creator to make all things new. He was sent to be a living sacrifice so that we might come back to that place of continual relationship with God the Father. His coming was foretold throughout the Old Testament. His death on the cross and His shedding of blood were necessary for our atonement. Being washed in His blood is our means of Restoration. We can be restored and made new only through our acceptance of Jesus the Christ and His sacrificial love.

Savor the pleasures of spring after a long and cold winter. God is a God of restoration. We can bask in His love and grace again. He made all things new. He renews and restores us back to His original plan for us. He created man for that personal relationship. We can again take long walks in the cool of the morning with God. Jesus the Christ, the second Adam, made it possible for us to be restored. The God of restoration knew what it would take to bring us back to that place. That place is truth and light. That place is our risen Lord and Savior, Jesus the Christ.

26

Good Luck, Lucky!

"Open your mouth wide and I will fill it" (Psalm 81:10).

"…give, and it will be given to you. A good measure, pressed down, shaken together, running over, will be put into your lap; for the measure you give will be the measure you get back" (Luke 6:38).

"Blessed are you who are poor, for yours is the kingdom of God. Blessed are you who are hungry now, for you will be filled. Blessed are you who weep now, for you will laugh. Blessed are you when people hate you and when they exclude you, revile you, and defame you on account of the Son of Man. Rejoice in that day and leap for joy, for surely your reward is great in heaven…" (Luke 6:20-23).

Well, he's flown the coop, so to speak! "Lucky" is the name we gave the little house wren that was hatched in the makeshift nest just over our porch swing. We gave him the name Lucky after pulling him out of both cats', Callie and Boots, mouths at least four times. There's no doubt in my mind that "lucky" is synonymous with "blessed." Had this little wren not been blessed beyond measure, we wouldn't have been on the front porch at just the right time in his little life to rescue him.

A revival preacher once said that absolutely everything we will ever learn is either about God or God's creation. I experience this statement as truth. Numerous are the occasions that I close my Bible after learning of God through His written Word, only to have His creation call out to me of yet another Truth that is our God. The Bible tells us that even the stones will cry out, and they do. I've written about everything from stones to birds. His creation proclaims His glory over and over and over again.

As I read the above Scriptures this morning, Lucky came to mind. We've watched him grow. We've watched him stretch open his mouth wide as mom and dad poked nourishment down his throat. He trustingly would poke up that wide mouth at the slightest movement of the nest, knowing that he was going to be fed. We've watched the flight lessons. Some were disastrous and required removing him from the virtual jaws of death. Nonetheless, he continued on in his journey to maturity and adulthood.

I don't know for sure the fate of Lucky, but I think maybe mom and dad moved him to the hanging fern which affords a little more privacy and safety. It may be that he's soaring high in a tree somewhere or frequenting a birdfeeder. Only God knows the fate of Lucky but God loved little Lucky enough to preserve his life at least four times and that gives me hope for Lucky's future.

God asks us to be as trusting and expectant as the birds of the air. He asks us to come as little children and as lilies of the field. He asks us to open wide our mouths, for He has so much good for us. Why can't we be as wise as the lily of the field and cast every worry and our cares upon Him? Why can't we come as little children, expectant and trusting and hanging onto every word because Daddy said so? Can't we be as wise as Lucky, and just trust that the God who showers down blessings like those above from the Mount of Beatitudes will provide and bless us beyond our vain imaginings?

He does and will bless us beyond our deserving. His mercy and grace abound to each of us. As we give unto Him, He promises to give back pressed down, shaken together and spilling over. Uncommon love, uncommon forgiveness, uncommon mercy, and uncommon grace are ours. We serve an uncommon God who loves us beyond all that we can ever desire or imagine. We're not lucky…we're blessed. Thank you, God, for loving us enough to allow all

Creation to glorify you so that we might see the Majesty of the God we serve. To You be all the glory and praise forever and forever.

27

Gotta or Unto, Your Choice

"Whatever your task, put yourselves into it, as done for the Lord and not for your masters, since you know that from the Lord you will receive the inheritance as your reward; you serve the Lord Christ" (Colossians 3:23-24).

"Commit your work to the LORD, and your plans will be established" (Proverbs 16:3).

"Commit your way to the LORD; trust in Him, and He will act" (Psalm 37:5).

Often I find myself saying that Biblical truth, "May all that I think, say, and do be unto the LORD." I say it sometimes without even realizing the words that are falling from my mouth. How many times do we utter words that are so imbedded in our spirits that we don't really hear the physical import of their meaning? Too often, I fear.

The busier life becomes, the more gotta days we experience. Do we find ourselves negatively spouting out, "I gotta go to the doctor, I gotta go to the grocery store, I gotta vacuum, I gotta change the beds, I gotta do this, and I gotta do that?" Of course I know that gotta isn't a word, but it certainly is a reality in today's busy schedules and life that is moving far faster than any of us care to admit.

Just look at your calendar and count those gotta days you have. We all long for those days where our calendar is blank and we can simply enjoy life as it comes without any busyness or interruptions that plague each of our lives in this twenty-first century. Those long, lazy days of our youth and years past are history. We live in a world that is spinning out of control. We're all living in the fast lane with someone or something honking just behind us wanting us to speed it up. Do more, do it faster, and get it done just so we can go on to the next thing.

Faster and faster we go toward what end? We are all simply victims of how we respond to this cyberspace world that we live in today. We have more home and kitchen gadgets than our grandmothers could have ever imagined. We have the miracle of electronics at our fingertips. We have all that could possibly be invented to make our lives easier and faster. Where is all that time that is saved by all this technology that we are so blessed to have?

The good news is that if you submit your priority time to the Lord, the time you are storing up is in eternity. Without God, that time you've saved is nonexistent. It's like that gerbil on a wheel. It's like water running through a sieve. It's worthless, meaningless, and unfulfilling. Flip that depressing thought and put the joy of the Lord into it. "Do all that you do unto Him and He will act," the Bible tells us. Jesus gives us all choices to make. We can choose life or death. We can choose good or evil, light or dark, happy or sad, health or sickness, we can choose. He gave us the opportunity to choose Him, not this world.

If we choose to do laundry unto the Lord today, He will give us His joy and His peace and we will be fulfilled in this small task that would otherwise be of no value. It's easy for even the unbeliever to see God in miraculous things that may occur, but it takes a believer to see God in the smallest of daily happenings. God is all-knowing, all-powerful, and ever present in the smallest of mundane experiences that we face. God is a God of miracles, but He's also the God of small things like lost glasses, phones ringing at just the right time, or a knock on the door. He's into our lives so much more than we give Him credit for and we should pray for the spiritual eyes to see Him at every turn.

We know that if God is in something, our burden is easy and our yoke is light. So, that being said, whatever your task might be today, do it unto Him. Choose this day to change your gotta into an unto and let God bless whatever you might be doing this day at home or office, and He will act. His precious word says so. May all that we think, say, and do be unto You, Father, of all things big and small.

28

Grandma Always Did It

"Then Job answered the Lord, 'I know that You can do all things, and that no purpose of Yours can be thwarted'" (Job 42:1-2).

Morning after morning, I've watched the three cardinals on their daily feast run at my bird feeder. I've finally figured out that although they are all the same size, two are adolescents and one is the parent. The two younger females land on the decking boards and wait for the adult to bring birdseed down and poke it into their mouths. They do some sort of quivering, fluttering of the wings as she approaches. It looks something like a feed me dance. I've enjoyed this display for a few days now and have wondered what sort of story or lesson I could learn from them. My thoughts have been that the adolescents appear to be capable of flying and eating on their own. Why didn't they just fly up the four feet to the feeder and feed themselves? They will peck and forage for seeds on the lower deck level but always wait for the adult to bring down fresh seeds.

My eye catches the beautiful geraniums hanging in the baskets under the eaves. As I break off the dried blooms, a couple of healthy sections break off from the plant. When I start to toss them away, I regret the waste of new growth. My immediate thought is that maybe I'll just try to root them; after all, Grandma always did it. There was the breakthrough to the story of the cardinals.

I learned so many things from my grandmother up until the day she went ahead. She always had jars and glasses full of rooting geraniums on her back sun porch. Whenever I smell the peculiar and inviting scent of a geranium, I think of my grandmother. She had such a green thumb and loved rooting her plants from breakings. She never had the luxury of running to Lowes or Home

Depot to buy lots of plants.

When I was younger, she taught me more about God, Jesus, the Bible, and life, in general, than any other individual that I can remember. She was always sharing her faith with me. My fondest childhood memories are of my Grandma Kirkman. I know without a doubt that she has been the single and strongest influence in my life. I don't believe that a day or two goes by that I can't recall a thought, action, or something that doesn't make me think of her. Little things like her humor, gentle conversations, her nurturing, and even her strong faith were fed to me on a regular basis. I learned from her, not only as a child, but as a young mother raising my own children.

I can remember all of my twenties were filled with visits to her house. I loved just being around her. I now see how much I emulate her in so many ways. She taught me things as simple as how to cut up a chicken for frying. She taught me things as complex as how to be thankful, even in adversity. Her favorite book of the Bible was Job. I thought this a strange choice when I was younger. Now in mid-life, I find that book not depressing, but encouraging, because of Job's strong faith and in how God rewarded that faith.

I learn from the cardinals that we continue to nurture our young long after the age of dependency. My grandmother's example feeds me yet today. She's been gone over twenty years. I can see lots of seeds that she poked into my heart continually sprouting, rooting, growing, maturing, and bearing fruit as I continue my faith journey to God.

We teach our young to walk, feed and dress themselves. We teach them all the worldly things they will need to know in order to survive. But none of us is going to survive this world. We must also sow seeds of faith every chance we can. God must be so integrated into our lives that we can show them, by example, the most valuable lesson of all. God is real. God is alive. God is present every day in every way. Instill God so deeply into our children's hearts that no matter what life throws at them, like Job, they will prevail. I know I can prevail; after all, Grandma always did it!

29

Great is Thy Faithfulness

"For surely I know the plans I have for you, says the LORD, plans for your welfare and not for harm, to give you a future with hope" (Jeremiah 29:11).

This great old hymn is on my heart this morning and I cannot stop humming and singing it. It was sung in last Sunday's service. As I've shared often, sometimes I get up with a song in my heart. Though I cannot sing well here on earth, I am convinced that I will sing in that heavenly chorus some day. God is a God of compassion and in His infinite mercy, He knows my love for music and will allow me one day to vocalize all the songs that He's put in my heart.

When my husband broke the news to me that his position at work had been done away with, our faith never faltered. Though shocked and frightened about the future, I repeatedly stated that the wind had been knocked out of our sails, but our boat was still afloat. God quickly came to us in so many ways to reassure us of His faithfulness. We remembered to remember His faithfulness, and that action gave us strength in a time of crisis, when before we would have crumbled.

After a battle with cancer, last year's tragic loss of three grandchildren in a car accident, and all the other things that God has been faithful to bring us through, we quickly determined that this was just a thing. This was nothing compared to what others were facing right now with the loss of spouses, sicknesses, and cancer treatments. This was not going to downplay all the good that is in our lives. We had each other and reasonable health, and that was more important than any career position.

The first thirty-minutes of our crisis together was interrupted by the phone. As we were teetering and trying to get our bearings about his job loss, that ring was just a nuisance that I could not bear. Rudely I answered, to find a Christian organization that I had been supporting on the other end of the line. I watch their program daily and have supported their efforts around the world. At this particular moment, I had no patience or inclination to answer a survey on what I enjoyed most about their programming. I quickly said, "The news, and I really don't feel like talking right now, because my husband had just lost his job and we are in the first few minutes of that trauma at the moment."

The girl on the other end of the line did not miss a beat, and offered to pray with me. I agreed and my husband picked up another phone extension as she went into a ten minute beautiful prayer. She lifted us up and requested that peace that surpassed all understanding to come to us at this horrific time in our lives. She included things that reminded me of God's faithfulness in the past. When I hung up, I knew that call, at that particular time, was God's continued faithfulness. I was already feeling His peace come into the situation.

Our discussions took on a whole new aspect and an upbeat spirit filled the room. Both my husband and I are facing a life changing time, but we are assured that God will remain faithful. He will open doors of opportunity that far surpass our expectations. My prayer time the next morning was fruitful, in that God quickly let me know that this time in our lives is just a change in direction. He gave us the above Scripture, not once, but through three different sources, the very next day. That's the way God works in our lives. He affirms, and then continues to reaffirm something just that way.

People seem not to be able to understand why we are joking and enjoying these days like some retired couple that have just come into those green pastures of retirement years. Things may get more desperate and we may falter along the way from time to time, but all things considered, we are positive. We are positive that the God we love and serve is faithful. "Great is Thy faithfulness...Great is Thy faithfulness...Morning by morning, new mercies I see." Like

Paul, we know how to be content with little or much. We know, "God's plans for us are for our good and not our harm and that He will give us a future with hope" (Jeremiah 29:11). Thanks be to our God who is faithful.

30

Heart's Desire

"May He grant you your heart's desire, and fulfill all your plans" (Psalms 20:4).

As I reflect this morning on the past year and try to envision the new year ahead, I'm struck by the thought that God has promised to grant my heart's desire. Of course there are numerous things that come to mind when I brainstorm for the desires of my heart. Renewed health tops the list. Closely behind come wealth, fame, and restoration of broken relationships. How very human the spirit becomes when offered limitless desires of the heart. I could probably compile a list as long as boredom would allow you to read. The new year ahead could be filled with desires as fresh and exciting as an unopened gift on Christmas morning.

Quickly the Spirit within me comes up with the perfect desire of my heart for me. My heart's desire would have to be, to be a good and faithful servant. How all encompassing that desire is. Thank you, Holy Spirit within this flesh, for coming up with a desire that could never limit God's awesome grace and mercy. That heart's desire could lead to more than I could ever hope for or dream up. To be a good and faithful servant is definitely my heart's desire for the coming year.

I pray that God will open the alabaster box within my spirit and pour His anointing onto the gifts that He has given me so that this servant might glorify the one true God. I pray that He will use those gifts and talents for His glory. I pray that He will use me to fulfill all of His plans for my life. I know through all of His promises that He will equip me and provide any provision I will need to fulfill His plans. God is so good. God is a God of provision.

I ask you to consider your heart's desire for the new year ahead. Pray and ask God what is in your alabaster box that could be broken open and poured out upon His throne. How could your talents or gifts be used to glorify God and help His plan for His kingdom? You just might experience the joy and peace that surpasses all understanding. You just might unleash the wellspring of the living waters that is bubbling inside you. Riches unimaginable await us all! Not the kind of riches that we can deposit in the bank but the riches that God's promises to give to us. "A good measure, pressed down, shaken together, running over, will be put into your lap; for the measure you give will be the measure you get back" (Luke 6:38).

Crack open your alabaster box today, petition God about your heart's desire and get out of His way! He's a shaker and a mover! He'll use you if you allow it. He'll grant your heart's desires in ways you might never dream up. Glory to God for all his goodness and mercy!

31

Hold Fast

"Not that I have already obtained this or have already reached the goal; but I press on to make it my own, because Christ Jesus has made me His own. Beloved, "I do not consider that I have made it my own; but this one thing I do: forgetting what lies behind and straining forward to what lies ahead, I press on toward the goal for the prize of the heavenly call of God in Christ Jesus. Let those of us then who are mature be of the same mind; and if you think differently about anything, this too God will reveal to you. Only let us hold fast to what we have attained" (Philippians 3:12-16).

What beauty feeds my eyes and ears! As I look up from my Bible, my gaze simply feasts on one lush and relaxing thing after another. Soothing balms for a weary spirit to indulge in this morning include: the crepe myrtle ready to bloom, the well watered sunflower bursting with life, the colorful array of potted plants scattered about, the bird feeders offering their wares to numerous birds, squirrels champing on sunflower seeds, a variety of aviary serenades offered up to heaven, and the soft reflections rippling atop the pool water. I have a virtual paradise just outside my back doors. How blessed can one individual be?

It's very easy to be spiritual and peaceful as I'm indulging myself in all this heaven on earth. I begin to notice assaults on my senses. Since we live on the backside of a motor sport complex, it's an almost daily occurrence to hear the roar of engines being tested for future races. The crane across the street cranks up and rumbles loudly as it pulls out of the driveway. New arrivals at the daycare next door chatter and squeal as they are dropped off for the day. Numerous distractions begin to poke holes in this otherwise Utopian scene. How can one be expected to meditate with all these distractions?

Eureka! I'll write about this Scripture and how we must hold fast to our peace whenever we go outside our comfortable spirit filled inner sanctum. I can enjoy the spiritual peace inside my fenced area, but, the rest of the world is outside this fence and not so serene or peaceful. There's always junk going on. Junk can also be defined as life going on. One of my hardest spiritual battles has always been how to hold my peace in the midst of life going on around me. Emotions, temper, anger, and many other negative things get in the way of my holding my peace all too often. God is definitely speaking to me this morning. Isn't this a great thing to share with others?

As I begin to write and really pull my thoughts together the phone rings. The orthodontist, wanting to clarify the office's mistake, rattles my nerves. Back to my thoughts and writing; the phone rings again. My husband wants to make sure I understand a time issue with a prescription that I'll need on vacation in the near future. Thoughts of having to hurry before it's time to pick up my granddaughter at dance meddle with my concentration. Okay, now, God, how can You expect me to keep my peace and write a worthwhile meditation with all this junk/life going on around me? Lighten up, God; I understand what You're trying to say to me this morning. How can a Christian easily keep their peace in the midst of "life" going on around us?

Each paragraph in this meditation ends in a question. As I reread the first paragraph, I focus on that question. How blessed can one individual be? That's the key to holding fast to my peace this morning. I have a real and personal relationship with the one true God who loves me and blesses me more abundantly that I could ever hope to deserve. That one true God is always ready to love me and bless me past any junk/life that comes my way. If I consider the things that He's already brought me through and done for me as the fenced area of my life, I can face the world outside that fenced area. He's proven to me time and time again that I can enjoy the peace of the spirit because He loves me enough to empower and enable me to face any distraction outside that which I've already attained.

We must press on because Jesus Christ has made us His own. We are His, and he will indeed give us peace to face life in its truest form, even if it comes as junk on a bad day. Never focus on the junk but hold fast to the Heaven on earth that He promises when we enter into His not our peace.

32

The Holy Way

"The wilderness … and rejoice with joy and singing … They shall
see the glory of the LORD, the majesty of our God. Strengthen the
weak hands, and make firm the feeble knees. Say to those who are
of a fearful heart, be strong, do not fear! Here is your God. He will
come with vengeance, with terrible recompense. He will come and
save you…A highway shall be there, and it shall be called the Holy
Way; the unclean shall not travel on it, but it shall be for God's people; no traveler, not even fools, shall go astray…but the redeemed
shall walk there. And the ransomed of the LORD shall return, and
come to Zion with singing…and sorrow and sighing shall flee away"
(Isaiah 35:1-4, 8-10).

Stand fast! Stand fast! Stand fast! This has repeatedly been God's Word
to me during my wilderness journey through sorrow and pain in the past year.
The sorrow has been comforted but the physical pain has been unbearable some
days. This unknown disease that has ravaged my body and baffled over a
dozen doctors; it has taken its toll on my physical body but never, for an instant,
so much as dented my Spiritual wholeness in Christ. I know first hand how
difficult it is to remain faithful in chronic pain. It's so hard to believe in miracles
when the pain takes the forefront of every thought. It's hard but not impossible.
God has continually let me know that He's right by my side. He's healed me in
the past and will again. He's assured me to be patient that my miracle is coming.

The whole armor of God donned daily, and sometimes numerous times throughout the day, has enabled me to withstand and stand firm on these evil days of chronic pain. God's Word tells me that He inhabits the praises of His people so I've made an extra effort to sing His praises during my worship time with Him each day. Praise and chronic pain are most definitely opposite ends of a spectrum. It's hard but, again, not impossible.

I've evolved from Biblical Martha to Mary. I've always known in the story of Martha and Mary that I was far too similar to the Martha Stewart/Biblical Martha type. I've always been too concerned with the fidgety preparations surrounding any given event. Anyone who knows me will testify to that fact. Everything has to be just so-so for the hostess with the mostest. I must say that I've already realized some of the good to come from this health episode has been the Mary time that I've had to spend at the Master's feet. Pain has given me time to study, read, and simply listen in His presence to revelation after revelation. The message that a cobweb here or a little dust there doesn't come into play with the real scheme of things has been received. Jesus Himself said, "Martha, Martha, you are worried and distracted by many things; there is need of only one thing. Mary has chosen the better part, which will not be taken away from her" (Luke 10:41-42).

I firmly believe this attack on my body has been a Satanic attack to slow me down. Satan knows that he can't win when it comes to God's plans, but he is able to thwart our headway and slow us down. He can attack with confusion, and unease in our bodies, which lead to diseases. He knows that he can't have me but he revels in the fact that he can play havoc with my life. He's really not even after me; he's after God's plans for me. His losing battle is with God not little old me.

It is written that our minds are his playground. It is written that he comes to rob, steal, and destroy. He knows that I belong to Jesus and he can't have me but he can confuse me into thinking that he's winning. My Spirit man refuses to submit to his wicked schemes. My shield of faith will thwart his fiery darts. It is written that I can speak things that are not as though they were. I can stand on God's Word and walk that Holy way talked about in this Scripture.

God's message to me this morning is to stay on that Holy way. He can find me there and come to my rescue more readily. Stand fast and let God go before me to fight the battles that I'm unable to fight myself is His word for me today. Stand fast! Stand fast! Stand fast! I'm standing fast on that Holy way. I am the redeemed of God, I am the ransomed of the LORD. I am the very sinner that Christ died for on Calvary. Come, Lord Jesus, and strengthen these failing hands and feeble knees. Come and show me that Holy Way where I can walk in victory! I rejoice with joy and singing. All praise and glory be to the living God.

33

The Home of God

"Then I saw a new heaven and a new earth; for the first heaven and the first earth had passed away, and the sea was no more. And I saw the holy city, the new Jerusalem, coming down out of heaven from God, prepared as a bride adorned for her husband. And I heard a loud voice from the throne saying, 'See, the home of God is among mortals. He will dwell with them; they will be His peoples, and God Himself will be with them; He will wipe every tear from their eyes. Death will be no more; mourning and crying and pain will be no more, for the first things have passed away.' And the One who was seated on the throne said, 'See, I am making all things new.' Also He said, 'Write this, for these words are trustworthy and true.' Then He said to me, 'It is done! I am the Alpha and the Omega, the beginning and the end. To the thirsty I will give water as a gift from the spring of the water of life. Those who conquer will inherit these things, and I will be their God and they will be my children...'" (Revelation 21:1-7).

The Bible tells us that a broken and contrite heart the Lord will not despise. God can use a broken and willing Spirit. Moses had to have had a broken and contrite heart to go from a prince in the palace of Pharaoh to herding sheep for forty years on the back side of a desert wilderness. I feel sure that he repeatedly asked God to put his broken life back together again.

I feel sure that when Joseph was cast into that pit before being sold into slavery, he begged God to also put his life back together. His prayers surely continued while in Potiphar's house as a slave, and later in prison for crimes he didn't commit. David implored God for restoration after he fell into the torment caused by his sinful nature. The Psalms are proof positive that David asked God to put his broken life back together again and again. On and on the Bible regales stories of people broken and put back together for God's purpose.

We all, most assuredly, in our lifetime, will come to a point that we will cry out to God to take our brokenness and put us back together as He sees fit. Reading this passage today, the realization struck me that God created us in our perfection when He created Adam in the Garden of Eden. Adam was carefree and innocent. Adam was happy!

Adam was created, not for any other reason, than to commune with and please God. He walked daily in the presence of God, naked and unaware of anything except his desire to please God and commune with Him. Before his fall, Adam knew no hatred, jealousy, wickedness, pain, sin or anything else that would take away from his perfect existence. Adam was God's perfect creation. He was a simple gardener in the perfect garden. He was content and happy because he was in the perfect will of God, his Creator. Then the fall!

God no longer walks in that perfect Garden of Eden that He created for Adam and Eve. The Bible tells us over and over that He lives in the hearts of believers. He has taken up residence in our earthly temples. We are His children and He is our LORD. This passage again confirms that truth.

The home of God is indeed among mortals and will be for all eternity. He comes into a shattered life or heart and puts all the broken pieces back together as was His original plan. "Nothing is new under the sun" (Ecclesiastes 1:9), the Bible tells us. The Garden of Eden and the new Jerusalem could very well be the same place. Heaven's description in Scripture so parallels the description of the Garden of Eden that we have in Genesis.

God's original creation for Adam could very well describe His final plans for us. He can put us together so that though we walk naked before Him;

we are unaware of it. Our sins, our infirmities, and our inadequacies are our nakedness and His grace can more than cover them with robes of righteousness. If we truly are walking with Him, those worldly things that could cause us pain are absorbed into His glorious light. Hurt, bitterness, sin and those things not from God are replaced with His peace that surpasses all understanding. God gave us Jesus as a living sacrifice to allow us to get to that place.

As servants to the God who lives with mortals today, we can continue to be His gardeners. We're no longer in that Garden of Eden filled with lush trees and fruits abounding but we are in the earth that is ripe for the harvest. We can allow God to use our brokenness for His purposes. We can walk with Him and allow our lives to be the home of God spoken of in this passage of Scripture.

Ask Him to move in today! Call the welcome wagon over to make Him feel at home! Open your life to His daily presence through prayer and reading of His word, and rest assured that He will not pass up the opportunity to move in! It is done! As it was in the beginning, it is and ever shall be, world without end, amen, amen.

34

Homeless Man

"In as much as ye have done it unto one of the least of these my brethren, ye have done it unto me" (Matthew 25:40).

A time my heart was strangely warmed was recently. I went into the homeless shelter to drop off my church's flour offering. While talking to the receptionist, a man came through the front door for help. He had a cigarette in his hand, had been drinking, and had not had a bath in quite some time. He asked to be put in "detox" so he could "get straightened out," as he put it.

There was something in the man's eyes that really warmed my heart. I took his hand in both of mine and greeted him very warmly and lovingly. I told him that it made me so happy that he was headed in the right direction. He kind of pulled back his hand and said, "You ought not be touching no one dirty like me; God loves you and God bless you."

I echoed right back at him that he should never forget that God loved him, too, and so did I. He smiled and said that he knew that for a fact because he had a "good God."

It warmed my heart much to know that even though he was drinking, the light in his eyes told me that he believed what he had just said. He spoke as though we might have different Gods, but it also warmed me to know that it's the same forgiving, loving God.

Just as He is with me as I go about my life at church, the market, or wherever I may be, God also is with this homeless old man, helping him struggle with alcohol and all the ills the world has cast upon him. "There but by the grace of God go I." My God and his God are one in the same and indeed a "good God." Thank you, Lord, for this blessed encounter.

35

I Will Hold Your People in My Heart

"...Then one of the seraphs flew to me, holding a live coal that had been taken from the altar with a pair of tongs. The seraph touched my mouth with it and said, 'Now that this has touched your lips, your guilt has departed and your sin is blotted out.' Then I heard the voice of the Lord saying, 'Whom shall I send, and who will go for us?' And I said, 'Here I am, send me'" (Isaiah 6:1-13).

When my friend left a message on the answer machine that another friend wasn't doing well and was discouraged, my spirits dropped. This friend and I had been in the same boat last year around this same time. We helped each by other joking that God had put us in the "same boat" for a reason. Sharing our fears and cancer surgeries seemed to lift both our spirits.

We both knew that God was holding us in His hands; yet, to share this journey with another in the flesh seemed to help in some way. God blessed me with two other cancer patients at this time also. Because we were all in the same boat, we bonded and nurtured each other. There was no room in our boat for self pity. God's blessings and praises overflowed throughout this circle of believers. Though we were all being touched with live coals, strength abounded. I attribute a large portion of my quick recovery to the prayers, faith sharing, and encouragement I received through these sisters in Christ.

As I went to God in prayer about my discouraged friend, fears overwhelmed me. I myself will be facing medical tests in the upcoming weeks and my first thought was, "Oh no, here we go again!" Though my tests will not be related to my cancer, the fear of cancer was quick to step into that cracked door.

God immediately quickened my heart to go to her. I felt the instant urge to cry with her. I wanted to pray with her. Whatever she wanted to do, I needed to share it with her and let her know that she wasn't alone.

Though God quickened my spirit to go where He led me, my flesh was consumed with fear and dread. This need struck too close to home for me. How could I be encouraging to someone else when I was using so much of my strength to lift my own spirits? I shared with my husband that I didn't want to go but I knew that I must. I tearfully prayed most of the afternoon for guidance and words of encouragement to share with this friend in her time of need. I felt guilt that her cancer was back and that mine was healed. Would she feel resentful of my complete recovery from the very disease that wouldn't let go of her? All these fears and more walked into that door left ajar for the evil one.

The times in my life that I've answered God's call to go have always brought me the sweetest joys. Until one has tasted these joys, there's no describing the sweet savor. It leaves you hungering for more. I can see that God's calls to go to distant lands and serve Him are somewhat easier than His calls to go and serve on the home front. He calls each of us every day to go. To go doesn't have to mean to travel a great distance. To go means to serve in whatever small way we can to accomplish His divine purpose for our lives.

When He said to go yesterday, after many struggles within myself, I went. How foolish I always am! By being obedient to His call, I received my blessing. The words flowed between this friend and me. She encouraged me. She lifted my spirits. God is so very good. We both were in agreement that God had assured us both of her recovery. Everything was going to be alright!

We sang one of my favorite hymns last Sunday as our church commissioned their youth group to go on a building team to Florida. This hymn has been on my heart all morning. To quote some of the lyrics, "I have heard You calling in the night. I will go Lord, where you send me; I will hold your people in my heart." Sometimes it's just that simple. Sometimes it's just that easy. To hold His people in our hearts and share their fears, their prayers, their faith, and their joys can be His call. I thank God for yesterday's calling. Because I was obedient and went where He sent me, my friend was able to answer her call. We held each other in our hearts and God blessed and loved us both.

36

Immediately

"...And He said to them, "Follow me and I will make you fish for people." Immediately they left their nets and followed him" (Matthew 4:19-20).

This is the Scripture that the pastor preached from just last Sunday at church. My husband and I were visiting a different church on a whim, but now I see that it was so that I could hear that particular sermon. His delivery was wonderful. He brought the Scripture into today by letting us imagine that Jesus would come down our street and to our door today.

He used himself as an example. He told the story of how he had received a call from the company who services his office copier. They call every so often and ask him to read off a meter number to them over the phone. This particular morning he was doing a number of church duties, preparing for a funeral, and most importantly working on taxes. When he received the call, needless to say, it was an unwelcome interruption to his business of the day.

When the girl at the other end of the phone asked if he could go into another room to read the meter, being perturbed, he just said, "No, I can't; I don't have time." Numerous times after that in his sermon, he would imagine Jesus knocking on his door and asking him to follow him and he would tell Jesus, "No, I can't; I don't have time today. I'm busy with church duties, preparing for a funeral, and I have to work on taxes."

This message hit me right between the eyes. He definitely was talking to me! God has spoken to me often with this phrase, "If you're too busy for God, you're busier than God wants you to be." After coming across that phrase a couple of years ago, I've learned to roll it around inside my head whenever I find it hard to say "no" to things. Whenever I'm unable to say no, I find that I overextend myself and get caught up into the busyness of church, friends, and family. These commitments always lead to obligations and duties that sometimes take precedence over God's calling me to immediately follow Him.

After coming back in April of last year from a building team trip, I was diagnosed with colon cancer. I had a colon resection, hysterectomy, and appendectomy this past summer. Needless to say, my life has been put on hold. This past year has been the best year of my life, yet the worst year of my life. God has blessed me with healing. I praise Him for answered prayer and early detection. For some reason, I've been dragging my feet about getting back into an active life.

In the past few years I've tried to tithe my time to God. My husband jokingly refers to me as a career volunteer. I have resumed a route for home delivered meals, help out with the district newsletter, and help out at the shelter, whenever I have time. Long ago God let me see that we all have twenty-four hours each day. How we use those twenty-four hours is up to each individual.

I am truly blessed in the fact that I no longer have to work. I know that some folks do not have as much free time as I do, but I lose patience with people who say they don't have time for daily devotion, Bible studies, volunteering, etc. We all have the same amount of time; it's up to us how we choose to use it. I have been dragging my feet about resuming my afternoon at the hospital and a few other things that God is convicting me of. After hearing this sermon, I tried to imagine Jesus knocking on my door and asking me to follow Him that day. I'd probably say, "Let me finish making the bed, doing the dishes, and I still have a little ironing to catch up on. I really don't have time today. Try catching me on a better day."

I know from past experiences that my sweetest days are the ones when I just make myself immediately available to Jesus, to do whatever He sees fit for me to do that day. After hearing that sermon on Sunday, I spent the whole day Monday doing little things I felt led by Jesus to do. The joys were abundant and I thank God for the opportunities He gave me. My household chores and everything else that I would have done on Monday were easily taken care of on Tuesday. That sermon was just the push that I needed, to get me back into the right thing for me to be doing for the kingdom of God. Thank you, Lord.

37

In the Shadow of Your Wings, I sing for Joy

"...My soul is satisfied as with a rich feast, and my mouth praises You with joyful lips when I think of You on my bed, and meditate on You in the watch of the night; for You have been my help, and in the shadow of Your wings, I sing for joy. My soul clings to You; Your right hand upholds me" (Psalm 63:5-8).

It's raining. We need this rain. It's been a while since we've had a good soaking rain. As I sit on my sheltered back deck, I'm blessed with such beautiful serenades. Even through the slow, relaxing downpour, the birds are singing their hearts out.

I watched earlier as they scurried about their morning scavenger hunts. That saying about the early bird catching the worm must have been foremost on each little bird's mind. I thought that they would hurry up and feed, then settle back into their individual nests or shelters to wait out the rain.

To my delightful surprise, there are about five different aviary concerts going on at this moment. How can those little creatures sing so fervently when I know that this downpour is pelting them? It's as though each little birdie is oblivious to his surroundings.

We must learn lessons from the nature around us. As I sit here with my hip hurting and the pain going down my leg, the suffering servant attitude settles on my brain. We must be thankful and praise God, no matter what befalls us. We must look beyond our surroundings and our flesh to the abundant life and joys that God blesses us with. He will take all our cares, aches, pains, disease, and sicknesses. The Bible tells us that by His stripes we are healed. He may not choose to alleviate our fleshly sufferings but I have all the faith in the world that He will give us enough grace to endure them.

Recently when I told a friend that last year's battle with cancer was the worst, yet the best, year of my life, she looked at me as though I had lost my mind. Unless one's love walk with God has reached that fail-safe point, there's no explaining the abundant grace that God showers on each of us to endure. A suffering servant knows that no matter what's going on around them, God is in absolute control of things. When the flesh cries out and the world crumbles around, God's grace will suffice.

I learned long ago the difference between being healed and being cured. To be cured of disease or sickness is only a fleeting, earthly thing. To be healed by God is an eternal, spiritual gift of grace. Like the birds that are singing this morning amidst pelting rains, I am blessed that I can sing for joy in the shadow of God's wings.

38

It Had to be Done

(John 19).

Tears flow as I read this chapter of some of Jesus' last hours on earth. Tears flowed the other night as I was blessed to witness the passion portrayed in a neighboring church's rendition of "Behold Him" for the umpteenth time. Tears flow any time that I relive that horrible passion of Christ in any way. I am very emotional and this age-old reenactment always squeezes the tears right out of my heart!

God has given me numerous insights as to why I weep. I mistakenly blamed a faceless they for years concerning Christ's crucifixion. How could they beat and scourge Him? How could they mock Him and scorn Him? How could they not recognize Him as the Messiah? How could they do all those atrocities to the one truly good person that God ever created? How could they?

Jesus was truly innocent and worthy as the Lamb of God to be sacrificed, that we might be reconciled to a loving and forgiving God. God, in His mercy, allowed the Truth to sink in one day, many years ago, that I am they. I reject the Son of God every time I speak a cross word with my neighbor. I reject Him over and over in countless ways whenever I don't live my life as God has ordained it. Unforgiveness, unlove, disobedience, or any other sin that I choose to commit puts me smack into the middle of that group of they.

God has blessed me abundantly with little pearls of wisdom that I know come only from Him concerning the passion of the Christ. Today, He's impressed upon my heart this simple fact. It had to be done. Whenever I weep and cry, why God, oh why, I'm assured that it was necessary. Jesus in the Garden at Gethsemane also wept and cried out for God to let this cup pass from Him. And yet, He quickly succumbed to God's will in the situation for God assured Him that it had to be done. It was the only way that there would be any hope of life everlasting for the rest of us and Jesus loved us that much.

It had to be done; otherwise, we would be lost for all eternity. He came for the sole purpose that it had to be done. Why so violently and cruelly did it have to be done? I don't have an answer to that yet but I do know now that it had to be done. Without a doubt, God had made provision for a weak and failing humanity to live forever in His holy Presence. Nothing we could ever have done would have reconciled us to Him. He had to provide a way for us and that Way was Jesus. He told us Himself, "I am the way, the truth, and the life everlasting" (John 14:6).

God also impresses upon me this morning that though it had to be done, we don't have to keep doing it. We don't have to crucify Jesus daily. Whenever we continue in the disobedience that God has pulled us out of, we continue to drive those nails into His precious hands. We continue to nail Him to that cross of death and despair. He conquered death that we might walk into that life everlasting right now, today. We can choose the light, and not the darkness, that is described in the first chapter of John.

Psalms 51 tells us that it's against Him and Him alone that we sin and do what is evil in His sight. Why do we continue with lifestyles and sinful natures that continue to hurt and reject the only One who ever loved us enough to change all of those things? Yes, God is impressing upon me this morning, it had to be done, but we don't have to continue doing it. A new creature, a new life, a new beginning is what the Resurrection is all about. A new way of life has been bought and paid for through Jesus' death on the cross for that old man that is in all of us.

He's alive! He's alive! He's alive! I say to all of you today to quit nailing Him to that cross where He's already finished His assignment. In His own words, "It is finished" (John 19:30). It had to be done, but it's forevermore a done deal. Don't let your hearts stay there at the foot of the cross with hammer in hand. Arise and go out into all the world and shout to the top of your lungs, He's alive, He's alive, He's alive! Glory to God!

39

It is Written

"...Then Jesus was led up by the Spirit unto the wilderness to be tempted by the devil. He fasted forty days and forty nights, and afterwards He was famished. The tempter came and said to Him, 'If You are the Son of God, command these stones to become loaves of bread.' But He answered, 'It is written, 'One does not live by bread alone, but by every word that comes from the mouth of God.' Then the devil took Him to the holy city and placed Him on the pinnacle of the temple, saying to Him, 'If You are the Son of God, throw Yourself down; for it is written, 'He will command his angels concerning You.' And 'On their hands they will bear You up, so that You will not dash Your foot against a stone.' Jesus said to him, Again it is written, 'Do not put the Lord your God to the test.' Again, the devil took Him to a very high mountain and showed Him all the kingdoms of the world and their splendor; and he said to Him, 'All these I will give You, if You will fall down and worship me.' Jesus said to him, 'Away with you, Satan! For it is written, 'Worship the Lord you God, and serve only Him.' Then the devil left Him, and suddenly angels came and waited on Him" (Matthew 4:1-11).

For the first time that I can ever remember, I feel threatened because I'm a Christian. Throughout history, people have been persecuted and even martyred for being a Christian. Here in the good old United States, we have always taken our religious freedoms for granted. We may or may not attend a church, we may or may not have a relationship with the one living God, or we may or may not read those dusty Bibles that decorate our coffee tables, desks, or dashboards. I can now picture the horror of not being able to own a Bible or read God's Word at my leisure. Some peoples have lived their whole lives, never having the option of opening the Bible and hearing God's personal revelation or invitation to each of us to become the children of the Great I Am.

In the back of my mind, I can remember good and faithful Christian people hearing some Biblical revelation and turning to each other to jokingly say, "Is that really in the Bible?" I've heard precious brothers and sisters in Christ confide that they really don't take the time to read the Bible as they know they should. I remorsefully begin to teach Scriptures like Deuteronomy 6 to my granddaughter. Scripture that should have been embedded in her spirit from the time she was an infant. God impresses upon me to teach my children and my children's children that, "I shall love the Lord my God with all my heart, with all my soul, and all my might" (Psalms 119:11).

In Mark 12:29-31, Jesus Himself reaffirmed this great commandment. When I see small children of other faiths shouting their beliefs into the news cameras, I'm ashamed. Though my children or children's children can sing sweet songs like "Jesus Loves Me," they cannot not recite precious Scripture that should be so ingrained into their hearts that they can immediately witness, defend or engage a discussion about their religious beliefs. One day they may have to witness to someone who has gone so far as to memorize his book of beliefs.

In Henry Blackaby's study Experiencing God he lists the ways in which we can expect God to speak to us. "God speaks by the Holy Spirit through the Bible, prayer, circumstances, and the church to reveal Himself, His purposes, and His ways," says Blackaby. If we are waiting to hear from God, we need to pick up the phone! Yes, we can see God in the beautiful flower, a kindly gesture, and the loving hand of a friend. Just think of all that we might be missing when we don't open our Bibles and allow Him to shower our lives with his abundant blessings and wisdoms to live by.

The above Scripture is very interesting in that Satan was also quoting Scripture to Jesus. Their whole dialogue dances around each one's knowledge of what is written. If Satan thought God's Word important enough to memorize in order to trip us up, we most certainly should deem it vital to protect ourselves from such evil. From childhood Jesus immersed Himself in the Holy Scriptures. Throughout his ministry, He prefaced most of what He said with, "It is written."

If we are truly to follow His example, we would do well to dust our Bibles and delve into God's Word. God's plan to impart knowledge and wisdom through His holy word can only be realized if we receive it. This Scripture shows me the importance of knowing for ourselves what is written. After all, if we follow the greatest command to love the Lord our God with all our heart, all our soul, and all our might, it stands to reason that we would want more than anything to spend time with Him in his Holy Word. My prayer today would be that God continue to reveal Himself to me through His Holy Word, and always impart His wisdom that I, too, might preface my personal witness with, "It is written…"

40

Jesus, Come Help Me With This

"My God in His steadfast love will meet me; my God will let me look in triumph on my enemies" (Psalm 59:10).

"For our struggle is not against enemies of blood and flesh, but against the rulers, against the authorities, against the cosmic powers of this present darkness, against the spiritual forces of evil in the heavenly places" (Ephesians 6:12).

Yet another crisis in this child rearing endeavor! Ever since we've undertaken the blessing/duty of raising our granddaughter, there has been one crisis after another. Oh, yes, there are many happy and good times in between, but it seems as she grows older, the crises are more frequent and more serious. I repeatedly tell myself, she's different, she's special, and she's not like other children. She has her own package of needs that demand more than most children. As she matures, those needs seem to stress us, stress her parents, stress her teachers, stress her bus drivers, and anyone else that is caught up in the strife that stresses us all to our limits.

Yesterday, the missing cell phone came to surface when the school bus driver poured out all that he had been dealing with concerning my granddaughter this school year. The cell phone had been taken away from her at least two or three times in the past few weeks. I was in stroke-mode, a term my daughter-in-law coined long ago, as I listened to him rail about all the inappropriate talk between her and others on the bus.

My cell phone, not hers, had come up missing a few weeks back and our fruitless searches through the car, house, garbage cans, etc. had taken a toll on both my husband and I. He had accused me of being neglectful in losing it. Much strife had been running rampant in our home because of the missing cell phone. Of course, when asked repeatedly, my granddaughter had denied any knowledge of the missing phone.

Our house was a virtual chamber of horrors last night. Punishments were doled out. Screaming and gnashing of teeth would best describe the scene coming down because of this latest development. Yes, she knows stealing is wrong. Yes, she knows lying is wrong. Why then, oh why, does she repeatedly steal and lie to the ones who are trying most to help her? Is it something that she can't help? Is it beyond her understanding that everything we own is hers for the asking? I don't think so, but I don't know for sure whether she comprehends there will be consequences for her actions. We must continue to discipline her whether we're sure she understands or not.

I could write about many lessons learned from this event but I'll focus on the one God put before me this morning. I allowed Satan to rob, steal, and destroy my peace. Forgive me, Lord. I didn't handle myself as a Christian. I all too quickly fell into his trap of losing my temper. He knows where my weaknesses are and hits me there all too often. Patience is a virtue that I have not mastered. Though I know what I should do, I always seem to do the wrong thing too quickly. Instead of venting my anger, I should have stepped back and focused on who the real enemy was at work in this strife.

God doesn't intend for us to handle everything with ease. He doesn't intend for us to have all the answers. He knows that He is in control, not us. He merely asks us to come to Him at a moment's notice and let Him have full reign in our lives. Instead of thinking, what am I to do over any given situation, we must quickly step back and cry, "Jesus, help me with this. I am weak and You are strong." Only Jesus is a match for our true enemy. This Scripture tells us that God will meet us and triumph over our enemies. He never expects us to do it on our own.

God, please help me to come to You more quickly with each and every trial. Let my first reaction to strife be that life affirming cry, "Jesus, come help me with this." That's why He's there, just a breath away, awaiting the invitation to step in. Let me never stand in the way of Your wisdom, understanding, and peace. Let me know from where my help comes. It comes from the Lord. Thank You, Jesus, for living in the here and now to help with every moment of every day.

41

Joy Comes In the Morning

"I will extol You, O LORD, for You have drawn me up, and did not let my foes rejoice over me. O LORD my God, I cried to You for help, and You have healed me. O LORD, You brought up my soul from Sheol, restored me to life from among those gone down to the Pit. Sing praises to the LORD, O you His faithful ones, and give thanks to HIS Holy Name. For His anger is but for a moment, His favor is for a lifetime. Weeping may linger for the night, but joy comes with the morning" (Psalm 30:1-5).

In spite of Emerson's theory about trees, there is nothing any more beautiful than a morning. The relaxed shadows cast by a rising sun, the birds singing with the urgency of the day, and even the crispness felt in the air of what will later be a hot, sweltering summer day are all parts of the beauty. Anyone who has ever risen to worship and praise in the early morning hours will immediately know the beauty of which I speak.

The day is like an enormous beautifully wrapped gift with all the excitement of the unknown thrown in. Before the world has had a chance to soil or mar the tiniest bit of its majesty is when we should seek God most fervently. Our road map, the Bible, repeatedly tells us to "Seek ye first the Kingdom of God and its righteousness" (Matthew 6:33). I take these pearls of wisdom literally this morning as I appreciate the beauty of the morning.

I've basked in the warming rays of the noonday sun. I've tremendously enjoyed what my husband and I refer to as our evening shade. I've praised and thanked my God under the miracle of a star-studded heaven with full moon that permeated a still night. All these are blessings that He pours out to us for our enjoyment during our busy lives. We need only to stop in the hustle and bustle to fellowship with Him, to be renewed and taste that sweet joy.

I realize that some schedules only allow an evening worship time. A time after all the day has come down upon us and we must turn to God to love and repair our Spirits. I've had those days also. But God repeatedly lets me know that my joy does come in the morning. If I seek Him early, He will give me the strength, peace, and yes joy to face the day head-on. His favor is indeed for a lifetime.

42

Keep Knocking

"And He said to them, 'Suppose one of you has a friend, and you go to him at midnight and say to him, 'Friend, lend me three loaves of bread; for a friend of mine has arrived, and I have nothing to set before him.' And he answers from within, 'Do not bother me; the door has already been locked, and my children are with me in bed; I cannot get up and give you anything.' I tell you, even though he will not get up and give him anything because he is his friend, at least because of his persistence he will get up and give him whatever he needs.' So I say to you, 'Ask, and it will be given you; search, and you will find; knock, and the door will be opened for you. For everyone who asks receives, and everyone who searches finds, and for everyone who knocks, the door will be opened'" (Luke 11:5-10).

After coming back from a getaway, I arose early today, refreshed and eager to catch things up from my absence. While watering the potted plants and moving things around so that the coming showers might also refresh my neglected ferns, I was dismayed to find that the little wren had finally nested in the fern on the front porch. I've spent most of this spring trying to discourage it from building its nest in that particular spot. Every year they try, and every year I have my reasons for not wanting them to nest there.

I immediately recall the above Scripture as I finally succumb to that little wren's persistence. I have torn up and thrown away at least four nesting foundations already in the past couple of weeks. Whenever a bird has built a nest in one of the front porch ferns, I find that I'm unable to water properly and move it around to different locations while away, etc. Eventually any fern that harbors a nest doesn't flourish like the other three ferns. Like the neighbor in this Scripture who already locked his doors and in bed with his children, I have valid reasons for not wanting a nest in those ferns.

If I can discourage the building of the nest, I don't feel as guilty; after all, there are numerous better spots to nest all around my yard. Once eggs are laid in the nest, I cannot bring myself to destroy those precious little capsules of life. Defeat over the territorial rights of that fern flood me as I spy four little eggs, neatly awaiting the life process. That wren took over the fern while I was away! A smile crosses my face as I say, "Okay, little birdie, your persistence has given you victory this spring! I'll grant you your proverbial loaf of bread this year simply because of your persistence."

Aren't we all constantly knocking and petitioning the Lord for this thing or that thing? I recall conversations of the past couple of days when my aunt shared that, after years of praying for the same thing over and over, she finally said, "Lord, You know what it is I want and need without me having to keep bringing it up." I'm the same way over certain prayers. Whenever we can't see or realize the answer to certain prayers, we are persistent in bringing them before the Lord on a regular basis. At times, I have even felt guilty about asking for something over and over and over. After all, my aunt is right, God knows what we need and want even before we ask.

The Bible tells us to keep knocking. We must keep asking. We must be persistent. Yes, God already knows what we need, but just maybe it's beneficial to us to keep knocking. This Scripture tells us that it's persistence that can eventually give us an answer to our prayer. Many witness' stories come to my mind as I meditate on this Scripture. Many stories have been told about someone coming to the Lord because a loved one had been praying for them for years. Answered prayers for healing, glorious miracles performed, and many a wayward loved one saved can be fruits of persistent prayer. I can recall many a person recant, "My grandma, my mother, my spouse, my friend prayed me into a relationship with the Lord."

Only God can call someone to Himself, but we can pray persistently that someone might answer that call. Jesus also tells us in the Bible that He is knocking at the door. We can be persistent to pray that others open that door. Once we have opened that door for Him and allowed Him to reign in our lives, we have a duty to be persistent about knocking on His door of prayer. Knock for your needs, knock for loved one's needs, knock for whatever is good, whatever is pure, whatever is holy. Knock for His will to be done. Knock, knock, knock, dear saints, and continue to knock.

43

Laughter

"But Jesus called for them and said, 'Let the little children come to me, and do not stop them; for it is to such as these that the kingdom of God belongs, Truly I tell you, whoever does not receive the kingdom of God as a little child will never enter it'" (Luke 18:16-17).

As the gentle breeze rustled through the leaves at the top of the huge maple, you could almost hear the laughter of a small child as it was being tickled. Then the breeze reached the top of the umbrella shaped mimosa tree. Oh what joyous laughter. As only God can make something as beautiful as a tree, only He can send the soft breezes to bring caresses of joy to His works of art.

Soothing laughter is a necessity to an abundant life. Many times in my life, I've felt the need to laugh. I'm talking about one of those side splitting, hiccup inducing, belly laughs. Those kinds of laughs always seem to alleviate any worries and relieve any stress that life uses to bottle up the human spirit. The expression, "laughter is the best medicine," had to originate somewhere. Since my grandchildren have come along, most of these doses of laughter usually follow something they have innocently said or done.

They beg Poppy to have a tickle fight just so they can laugh and plead for him to stop. Maybe this is part of the reason we should come into God's kingdom as little children. A child is rarely stressed out or worried. They have an innocent faith and can laugh easily at a silly face or express unlimited joy at a tickle bout. If we come as little children, we, too, can experience the joy that comes from a gentle breeze. We can laugh out loud as the wind kisses our cheek and tosses our hair. God's abundant life is everywhere around us. We must not complicate things by searching too hard for it. We must come as a small child and simply enjoy it all around us.

44

Let's Talk

"The LORD spoke to Moses face to face, as a man speaks to his friend" (Exodus 33:11).

As I read my devotional this morning I'm reminded that conversation is a two step endeavor. I talk; you listen...you talk; I listen. All too often I fall back into that habit of doing all the talking during my prayer time. I know from years past that this is one of the hardest habits to break in my spiritual discipline.

We tend to take all our concerns to God, and rattle off what we need and who we want to lift up to Him. We must sound like one of those speakers at Sonic. From God's end it has to be humorous to hear, "I'll take a healing, a good day, anything that You see fit to throw into the bag, and, oh yeah, give me a little peace and understanding today also; and by the way, can you supersize that order?"

Of course we understand that God knows all our concerns and needs before we ever lift them up to Him. He has given us the gift of prayer, possibly to remind us to listen to ourselves as we talk to Him. We must never forget the quiet time required of our conversation with God. A quiet time, with hearts in communion with Him, allow Him to speak to us so that we might hear Him more clearly.

I find, when I'm in the give and take relationship that I have with God, I see Him in most everything that I encounter during my day. That's the listening end of prayer. Whenever I feel that I'm not seeing God in something, I simply have to get still and allow Him the opportunity to speak to me. That still, small voice within each of us must be allowed access to our busy, hectic, daily lives. It takes discipline and practice. It's so very easy to lose that contact because of busyness, distractions, or even our unwillingness to listen.

We are to be constantly in prayer with God. That's the relationship that matters in each of our lives more than the breath in our lungs. The conversations we have with Him all during the day must be allowed fruition. We talk; He listens...He talks; and we listen. It's those two steps again that qualify a conversation between two parties.

I'm reminded by my devotional time this morning to complete the second half of that conversation. When I say, "God, let's talk," I must be quiet and listen to His still, quiet voice. As Elijah found out on the mountaintop, God wasn't in the great wind, the earthquake, or the fire. God was in the sheer silence. The silence requires an action on our part. Sometimes, just to be still and listen is the greatest action we can take.

45

Living in His Shadow

"You who live in the shelter of the Most High, who abide in the shadow of the Almighty, will say to the LORD, 'My refuge and my fortress; my God, in whom I trust'" (Psalm 91:1-2).

As I meditate on this cool winter's day, I'm able to sit outside, with the warmth of a sweater, and gaze upon God's creation. The blue sky mingles with jet streams and random clouds. The sun is bright and warm upon my face in direct opposition with the chill in the air that stings with icy fingers. God's world is His idea, His imaginations, and His creation. All that we know and that our fleshly senses might experience are but manifestations of God's Word that has been handed down and evolving since that creation moment described in Genesis. "In the beginning, God created…" (Genesis 1:1) starts His holy Word to each of His children.

All that we know, all that we might experience is but a shadow of His almighty plan for man. As I continue to meditate, my eyes spy two towering sycamores in the back yard that are finally deplete of all foliage and have taken on that wintry appearance of spiked fingers reaching heavenward, resting until renewal and springtime. What catches my attention is that one is growing completely in the shadow of the other. Its trunk seems to parallel the older tree. Its height appears equal to the more mature sycamore, and it is just as healthy and vibrant in bark tone. Yet, my common sense lets me know that it's always been in the shadow of the older tree. How can it be so healthy?

Sunlight is vital to growth, maturity, and health of plants and trees. How could this younger tree have survived living in the shadows? How could it be so healthy and every bit as sturdy as the older one? Then this Scripture comes to mind. Psalm 91 is a Psalm of promise, comfort, and protection. It continues to say that God will deliver and protect those who know His name. When they call to Him, He will answer and rescue them and honor them. With long life, He will satisfy them. Those who live in the shadow of the Almighty LORD are shielded and protected from the terror of the night and the arrow of the day.

Living in that kind of shadow is imperative! It's totally essential to a child of God to be in His shadow and under His protection at all times. We live in a hurting world but this world is also a hurtful world. God will shield us from many things that would wound and deter us from being about our Father's business. He will command His angels to guard us in all our ways. What assurance and promise that part of this Psalm gives each of us. With God covering us with His pinions, His protection, and His army of angels, what do we have to fear? Nothing! Nothing, not even death, can separate us from God's love and protection.

Brothers and sisters in Christ, take heart, and be of good cheer. Your God is shielding and protecting you from whatever it is that might be coming up against you today. He's got your front and His army of angels has your back. Live in His shadow today. Live under the pinions of the one who loves you like a mother hen. Live the life that God wants for you and has imagined from the beginning of time for you, His child. He thought of you and imagined life for you; take comfort in that, and know your importance to the God of all creation. He wants good for you. He desires that you prosper and be in health. He loves you and is shading you from all harms. Live in His shadow and enjoy the abundant life that He desires for you today!

46

The Mockingbird

"He put a new song in my mouth, a song of praise to our God. Many will see and fear, and put their trust in the LORD" (Psalms 40:3).

In the past few years, I've developed a special fondness for watching birds. My backyard birdfeeder has become a highlight of my devotional times spent with God. It's right there in front of me as I read God's Word, and many a morning my prayer times have been interrupted by the delightful intrusions of my aviary friends.

This morning, the new mockingbird that has taken up residence in my neighborhood serenades me. I know he's new to the area because he has a new song that has caught my attention many times. Oh, we've had mockingbirds, but this new guy has a much more extensive repertoire. He twills, calls, chirps, and charms my spirit with the most glorious of songs. His uncommon song reminds me of some tropical paradise backdrop. His rich tone and variety of sounds is nothing short of miraculous. I'm entranced each time that he begins his symphony.

As he sings, twills and warbles this morning, I reflect on our individual journeys along life's path. Do our lives portray the new song written about in the above Scripture passage? Do others readily hear our new song of praise to God? God intersects each of our lives in a most unique way. We each have a testimony unlike anyone else's testimony. There may be similarities because of life's common thread of trials and tribulations, but God reaches out to each of us in His own unique plan for our lives. We each have a gospel or good news that is unlike anyone else's experience.

He made each of us unique, and yet our songs sometimes simply mimic the songs of others. Do we sing of His praises, as we know Him? When we become one in Christ, our songs meld into the songs of others much like that mockingbird with his unfamiliar song. Our contribution to the whole symphony is our personal encounter with the living God. Our particular warble or witness just may be the one that will bring someone else into the Kingdom of God. We must always sing our own song along with the testimony and songs of those we meet along the way.

Eventually we'll be singing that glorious song for all eternity. We'll be like that mockingbird. We'll be singing to the God Most High forever and ever. His creation sings His praises each day. The birds of the air regale His glory. Sing His praises, oh child of God. Sing your new song...The children of God cry Holy, holy, holy is the Lord God Almighty.

47

Much

"...from everyone to whom much has been given, much will be required; and from the one to whom much has been entrusted, even more will be demanded" (Luke 12:48).

This particular Scripture has played in my mind over and over in the past few months. Though the context of this parable is completely contrary to the message God is quickening in my spirit, I finally think that I am grasping what He's been trying to say to me. The Living Word of God speaks in many different ways and on so many levels. Every reader of the Bible would be quick to agree that the same Scripture says different things to them, depending upon the need or the situation. I know personally that God's Word, when read with the Holy Spirit there to interpret it, takes on many avenues of wisdom, depth, and understanding.

I've always prayed for faith and for God to help my unfaith. I have much more faith today than I had yesterday. Faith is something that is definitely a gift from God. I can remember many years ago trying to understand the concept of faith. It's not only a noun; it's a verb requiring us to faith as an action. Faith is something that unless you have it, it's nearly impossible to wrap your mind around. Yet, faith is the easiest of all God's gifts to accept. The day I received the breakthrough that I don't have to understand every thing or be able to explain God's mysteries, but to merely accept with faith that He is God and in control, my struggle with understanding faith ceased.

Faith is not some medal or award for being a Christian. Faith isn't something that the scholars can be awarded after years of study. Faith isn't anything that is attainable through any endeavor of our own. Faith is simply coming to God with the trust of a child. Faith allows Him to be Father God. Faith allows us to fall helplessly into His powerful arms and curl up like a small child and enjoy a nap the rest of our life on this earth. Faith is something that grows and blossoms through our many struggles and difficulties that we face during our lifetime. Faith comes through patient suffering, as described in Romans 12:12. I've had other Christians remark that they wished they had my faith.

I would never presume to flaunt my faith but I am aware that God has molded me into a woman of strong faith. We've all been given the same faith that is the size of a mustard seed. It's that action part of faith that stretches it and grows it into that giant tree that comes from the tiny mustard seed. My faith has come with a price. Loss of my first child, divorce, estranged family, cancer, and now the loss of grandchildren to a horrible car accident are just a few of the price tags that it cost to stretch and grow my faith.

When I was knit in my mother's womb, God ordained that I would be that grandmother that would suffer this horrendous loss of grandchildren. Before I ever conceived their father, God knew that faith would bring me through this greatest time of trial. Not for one moment have I doubted that God was in control in the aftermath of this accident. I've been given much faith from my Father God and now that I'm required to face this tragedy, I faithfully crawl up onto His knee and let Him carry the pain, the loss, and the heartache. He knows from experience and can show me the compassion necessary to get through this trial. God has given me much faith and now, more than ever in my life, much faith is required. He's telling me through His holy Word to continue on with my faith. He's telling me to stretch it and to grow it, for it will allow me to endure. The old saying, "He'll never put more on you than you can stand" comes to mind this morning. This has to be the hottest fire that I've been thrown into Father God. Thank you for my faith and please help my unfaith.

48

My Garden Place

"In my Father's house there are many dwelling places. If it were not so, would I have told you that I go to prepare a place for you? And if I go and prepare a place for you, I will come again and will take you to myself, so that where I am, there you may be also. And you know the way to the place where I am going" (John 14:2-4).

As I spend time with God this morning, He reminds me of that old hymn about the mansion just over the hilltop that my Daddy always sang as I was growing up. I can hear his rich baritone voice yet today, singing it all throughout my younger years. He wasn't always the example of Christian love, but he left his whistling and singing of certain hymns deeply and fondly embedded into my childhood memories. My Dad, uncle, and aunt used to sing gospel hymns on the radio in their younger years and the memories always flood back of my father whenever I hear that old hymn. Those tears of mine that God captures and puts into a bottle are always replenished whenever that old hymn comes on the radio or is sung in church.

Often, I've cried out to God about my mansion or place that He's preparing for me. I've constantly petitioned that my mansion or room be an outside garden spot. I feel closest to God whenever I'm in my special garden spot where we meet each day that the weather allows. It's heaven on earth for me. I constantly remind God that since I must spend eternity in my prepared place with Him, that I would be happiest outside in the sunshine, fresh air, flowers blooming, and birds singing. No matter how foolish this request may sound, I know that God will grant my heart's desire, and that as far as I'm concerned, my mansion, place, and/or room will be a garden spot that rivals none other. He's preparing a place for me where I can spend eternity with God the Father in mutual love and adoration of Him and all of His creation.

This morning, I'm quickened to the similarities that our heavenly home might have with our life here on earth. I've heard it said, "We make our own 'happy.'" Within reason, our lives are what we make them. We can choose daily to be happy or sad. We can choose daily to do good or evil. As I've matured in my Christian life, I've come to realize that most of the evil can be found within my own heart and life. A daily prayer for the Holy Spirit to shine its light into every corner of my mind, heart, and life dispels any darkened corner where evil might lurk, rear its ugly head and take root.

Life is about choices and we make our own choices as our free will gift from God. We can choose to do the right thing or the wrong thing. The power that God gave us whenever He gave us freedom of choice can often make the difference between a happy life, or one filled with remorse and sadness. Although we often revert to that old, "the devil made me do it," we must take responsibility for our own choices. We choose to sin and be apart from God. No one tempts us or makes us, it's our freedom of choice to do right or do wrong. We do have a loving Father who forgives all our sin and loves us in spite of our wrong choices.

I've met folks who aren't going to be happy no matter how much God blesses them, and then I've met those who are happy in the Lord in the midst of all kinds of calamities. The only difference that I can see is their choice of how they handle the life coming at them. Life happens to all of us each day. Life is raining down sickness, job losses, and separation from loved ones, death, and all sorts of things that are simply part of the life process. Our pastor spoke Sunday of God raining down blessings and grace upon us. God's torrential outpouring of grace is far beyond anything life has to drizzle at us. We simply must make the right choice to see the good in all things, even that potential bad thing that might be going on in our life today.

Life requires the gardening skills that each of us has been given. Garden spots require constant weeding. Heavy rains, whether torrential or drizzles, water not only the flowers, but also the weeds. It's a daily life process that we must constantly be nurturing our spirits and making right choices to thwart the growth of any weed found there. Small seeds of unforgiveness or unlove could grow into gigantic problematic weeds. It's best to uproot them while small and tender enough to easily pull out.

Look for the good in all situations. Make a positive right choice to see God in all things going on. He, after all, is in control of all things. Our Bibles tells us that, "All things work for the good of those who love the Lord and are called according to His purpose" (Romans 8:28). Our heavenly home is part of our inheritance that is imperishable, the Bible tells us in I Peter. It's kept in heaven for us, who are being protected by the power of God through faith, for a salvation ready to be revealed in the last time.

If you indeed have tasted that the Lord is good, continue to feast upon His grace that rains down and choose to be happy, not sad; choose to do good rather than evil, and know that Jesus is coming again to take you to where He is. Your heavenly home is being prepared, but you must be vigilant in this life-time to make it the best that your choices will allow. Weed where weeds pop up, be the best person that God created you to be and know that God will take care of all the rest. We all know the Way and His Name is Jesus. He's gone to prepare a place for us; perhaps mine will be my garden place.

49

My Silky

"She had heard about Jesus, and came up behind him in the crowd and touched the hem of His garment, for she said, 'If I but touch His clothes, I will be made well'" (Mark 5:27-28).

Most of us know well the story of the hemorrhaging woman who dared to touch the hem of Jesus' robe. In the midst of the crowd, she sneaked a healing touch. Yet, Jesus felt the power go out of Him and knew that someone had dared to approach Him for that healing touch. How powerful this story is for those of us who plead and pray daily for a healing touch. Jesus, though hustling through the crowd, was brought to a halt and responded to the faith of this woman.

My son used to have an old blanket that gave him security until he was six or seven years old. The tattered silky edge of that blanket healed any worry, boo-boo, or fret that he encountered in those first few years of his life. Many years later, two of his children inherited that sweet dependency on their "silky." My grandson and granddaughter both had to have a piece of my old satin/silk pajamas to quiet themselves before going to sleep.

They would rub the silky on their cheeks and you could actually see the soothing sedation of its touch engulf them. I had encouraged their love for the silky by ripping up those old pajamas and sending strips home and also keeping some for my house.

Both children never took a nap or went to bed without the security of their silky. There were times when we searched for a lost silky with fear and trembling. That dependency on such a small thing is human nature in all of us.

We all have certain things that seem to soothe and secure us in times of dread and fear. It could be a cup of hot tea. It could be cheesecake. It could be a close friend. It could be anything that takes the edge off of uncertainty and the unknown.

As I lift my hands heavenward in my daily surrender to Jesus, I reach for the hem of His garment. My mind's eye tries to visualize my hands touching that divine robe worn by my security blanket. Jesus is the silky of this middle-aged, tattered Christian. Jesus is my soothing balm in time of need. Jesus is my soft touch against a tear-stained cheek. Jesus is the answer to any worry, boo-boo, or fret that might come my way. Jesus, the great Redeemer, will hold me fast against any dread or fear.

I ask you what it is that you turn to in time of desperation and need. We all have those trials in our lives that render us helpless and totally dependent on something other than ourselves. Where do you turn? Whose name do you call out? I call out to my one secure and constant, Jesus, for just a touch of the hem of His royal robe. Just a touch of that imaginary silky relieves any hurt, disease, or troubled thing in my life. My Vine, my Way, my Lord, my Friend, my Brother, my Bread, my Life, my Light, my King, my Jesus, my Silky. Thank you, Jesus, for being all things to me, your servant girl.

50

Not Far

"…though indeed He is not far from each one of us. For in Him we live, move, and have our being…" (Acts 17:24-31).

We need only to seek and we shall find, the Bible tells us. I'm puzzled as to why so many people can live their entire lives and never see, or only catch glimpses, of God. Some feel that God is this austere deity that we must never approach in a familiar way. My personal relationship with God is completely opposite. Whenever I make myself open, I can see Him in most everything around me.

He's all around, in and through our every moment and every breath. He's in the flower as it pushes up from darkness, grows, and then blooms with such vibrant and colorful beauty. He's in the clouds as they mystically move, change shapes, and soften the sky. God is in the birds of the air as they sit perched on a limb to sing, warble or chirp with such pleasing sounds. God is in the gentle breeze that caresses our cheek or blows tendrils of hair to tickle our face.

God is the Creator of all life in us and around us. Since He created us for His pleasure, why would He work His creation miracle, only to go off some-where to not enjoy His craft? I just know that in spite of our iniquities, God is a hands-on creator. He's in our midst leading, guiding, and enjoying His hand-iwork. I feel that He takes pleasure whenever we do see Him in the smallest of things.

I also think it's probably easier to see God working miracles in major life events. But, to see Him in a needed hug from someone is to know He is near. To see God in something as simple as a minor delay and then finding out later that you avoided a major accident because of the delay, is to know He is near. I can see God in something as small as finding a lost dog after frantic prayer. We must seek Him in all things large or small and we will find Him. This Scripture tells us He is not far from each and every one of us. He's never far; we need only to open our hearts and eyes to see He is near.

51

Not the End of the Story

"They said to one another, 'Here comes this dreamer. Come now, let us kill him and throw him into to one of the pits; then we shall say that a wild animal has devoured him, and we shall see what will become of his dreams'" (Genesis 37:19-20).

Do you suppose that when Joseph was stripped of his lovely coat of many colors and thrown down into that dank, dirty old cistern that he just maybe thought, this is the end of my life? I try to imagine what he must have felt to have his own flesh and blood turn on him as they did. It would be bad enough to have had strangers do this awful thing to him, but the knowing that these were his own brothers must surely have worsened the impact of the whole ordeal. As if throwing him down the well to die weren't enough, they went so far as to sell him into slavery. Some things can be worse than death. As we all know, this was not the end of the story.

Joseph never faltered in his devotion to his God. Even when life seemed at its worst, Joseph continued to worship and have faith that his life was in God's hands. The Bible leads us to believe that he never doubted that God had a plan for him. Indeed, the well, and even slavery, was not the end of the story for Joseph!

God saw fit to raise Joseph to a position that would eventually benefit the whole nation of Israel, such as it was at that time. Though nation may be too strong a word to use for the twelve sons of Jacob and their families, they indeed were the beginning of a nation. Joseph's untimely and unwilling journey into Egypt laid the foundation for the history of Israel, the nation. Though it would be many years until the eventual bondage, slavery, and then exodus of the descendants of Jacob—*that was not the end of the story.*

All Christians know the story of the life of Jesus Christ. The betrayal, the abuse, the crucifixion must have seemed to be the end for some of those followers who witnessed such atrocity. Praise God in all His glory that that, too, was not the end of the story. On the third day He arose, and that is why we, each and every one, can face any and all trials in our lives, and know that no matter how severe or harsh circumstances are, that it's not the end of the story.

As long as we have breath to breathe, we can rest assured that God is working His plan for our lives just as it should be. No matter what fearsome thing we may face, God will use it to lead us into His will for us. He has given us example after example in the stories of the Bible, especially this particular story of Joseph. We can never see the whole picture, only one frame at a time. So, no matter the frame your life may be in at this moment, be encouraged by knowing that it's not the end of the story!

52

Oh Magnify the LORD!

"I will bless the LORD at all times; His praise shall continually be in my mouth. My soul makes its boast in the LORD; let the humble hear and be glad. O magnify the LORD with me, and let us exalt His name together. I sought the LORD, and He answered me, and delivered me from all my fears. Look to Him and be radiant; so your faces shall never be ashamed. This poor soul cried, and was heard by the LORD, and was saved from every trouble. The angel of the LORD encamps around those who fear Him, and delivers them. O taste and see that the LORD is good; happy are those who take refuge in Him" (Psalm 34:1-8).

So safe, so sure, such a refuge is my morning place. Just outside my back door, I go for a safe sanctuary to commune with the God of all Creation. He meets me there to encourage, to comfort, and to lift me up to heights of glory that only being in His presence can afford any of us. I've tasted and indeed the LORD is good.

As I gaze upon the flowers, the beauty and the worldly comfort that God has blessed me with, I thank Him. I take refuge here in this place that is familiar and safe for me. I've planted, weeded, watered, and nurtured all that my eyes can see and thank God humbly for His key role in all my blessings.

It makes me feel good to sit our here in the cool shade of the morning and sip an extra cup of coffee before going to the Lord in meditation and prayer. This is the beginning of each and every day of my life, and it is indeed good. God's grace allows me this time to be with Him, and I give Him thanks and exalt Him for this abundant blessing.

As my eyes dart from familiar thing to familiar thing, I realize that it's not this place that I take refuge in. I know how quickly a storm approaching can blow everything about. Cushions are in the pool, balls under the deck, and umbrellas can soar over the fence and into the neighbor's yard. Disarray can come at any moment and this Utopian setting can look like a disaster area. My safe sanctuary is in the spiritual realm, not the worldly one.

So it is with our lives. God is our refuge. He is our safety net and fortitude in times of disaster, trials, and trouble that can plaque our lives at any given moment. His grace and mercy resides in the heart that magnifies Him and praises Him for all the goodness that comes from knowing Him and accepting Him as Lord and Savior.

As this Scripture says, "Look to Him and be radiant" (Psalms 34:5). Look to Him today with all that you might be going through and enter into His rest, His peace, and His presence. Seek Him and magnify Him for indeed His word tells us that He is not far from any of us. He "encamps around those who fear Him and delivers them" (Psalms 34:7). He delivers us from all that might be raging tempests blowing our lives about; His precious word says, "Taste and see that the LORD is indeed good" (Psalms 34:8).

Take refuge in Him this day and go forth to be happy. God wants His children safe and happy and He's ever present in times of need to supply. "Let His praises be continually in your mouth," this Scripture says. That sweet savor of praise and thanksgiving that tastes more succulent than any morsel that you might ever put in your mouth. Magnify the LORD! Exalt Him! Be safe and take refuge in His safe sanctuary today!

53

On the Road Again

"Jesus said to him, 'I am the way, and the truth, and the life. No one comes to the Father except through me'" (John 14:6).

Life is but a journey down a busy expressway! As I sit here spending a few moments with God before I start my busy day, my gaze goes to the hotel window. The drapes are drawn, except for about ten inches of white gauzy sheers that cover the small gap between the heavy drapery materials.

I hear much traffic, and through the veiled opening I can see two distinct traffic patterns. The upper lane of traffic is zipping by at high rates of speed; the second lane pattern is slower. Before I open the sheer curtain, I already know from my journey here the night before that the busiest traffic are vehicles zipping south on a busy interstate, with destinations and agendas in mind.

As they speed down the highway, their minds are ahead of them toward their destinations. The next level of activity is the off-ramp, fewer cars and trucks, traveling at a slower pace as they exit the busy highway. When my view is unobstructed by the sheer's veil, I spy a third avenue of travel. The backside of the parking lot of this hotel is virtually empty. It's definitely a road less traveled.

Comparing the three roads to the way we can opt to live our lives is prevalent to me this morning. I tend to take the bottom road, less traveled. It's safe and quiet; it's behind the busy hotel and free from invasive or uncomfortable traffic or activities. I realize that although it has inviting characteristics, the most important aspect of this path is that it goes "nowhere."

The off-ramp, though much busier, is still leading away from the main stream of traffic and activity. Its vehicles are either at their journey's end or stopping to refuel or in some other way preparing to get back onto the busy interstate.

Many times in my lifetime, I've found myself on the off-ramp of life. Needing to commune with God, rest, or otherwise prepare myself for the road ahead. Spending time with God always prepares us to face the hustle and bustle of high volume life happening and the open road ahead. Though necessary, it's very dangerous to stay long on an off-ramp.

The highway or open road is the only real place to be. It's where life is happening. Multitudes of faces are going somewhere! That well traveled road of life leads to all our final destinations after our earthly lives. Some may fall victims to temporary mechanical problems, road rage, or even multi-car pile-ups. We never really know what awaits us down the road. The slim chance of anything like that happening should never prevent us from the road trip. Compared to the hoards of people who reach their final destinations, any road hazard that may or may not befall each of us is far greater.

Jesus is truly the way and our path. We need not fear the traffic jams, weather conditions, or any other delay along our way. He gave us our road map, the Bible. He is right beside us to lead us through the hazards. Ultimately, life is going to "happen" to all of us. Good or bad, it's our cup to drink from, and we can make of it what we may. We can experience life more fully while we're in the traffic pattern than on the backside of any parking lot. I can hardly wait to get on the road again.

54

One Drop

"On that day living waters shall flow out from Jerusalem..."
(Zechariah 14:8).

The pool of water that is dripping from the glass tabletop over and down onto the decking boards is left over from last evening's flower watering. A slow but steady drip is taking place. The water in the plate sized pool on the table wells up next to the edge, then drops, one drop at a time, down onto the decking boards below. Slowly a pool of water about the size of a saucer is forming. It seems a slow process, but gravity is moving the water pool.

As Jesus in Heaven allows us to drink from His well of living waters, we can only consume one drop at a time. Many drops will eventually form a pool of drops. Whenever our drops of the living water fill us with blessings, joys, and the fruit of the Spirit, those gifts well up inside of us until some eventually spill over onto others. I think this is God's divine law of gravity.

Personally I always find myself gravitating toward those persons who are Godly, joyous, and full of the Holy Spirit. I find that if I hang out with people like this, quite often some of their Spirit-filled joy rubs off on me. God instills in us a hunger and thirst for more of Him. Along with personal time spent with Him by reading our Bibles, prayer, and worship time, God instills in each of us a desire and yearning to commune with Him and others on that same journey.

Fellowship with other Christians is necessary to fill our pools with living water. One drop at a time, water is a thing easily wiped up and overlooked; but many droplets pooled together can be a forceful thing. Floodwaters that surge along a path of destruction began with one drop of water. The force of moving waters, which also began as one drop at a time, powers electric generators.

Recently I was again blessed to be able to visit Niagara Falls. Anyone, who looks upon the wonder of these horseshoe shaped falls, simply must acknowledge that there is indeed an almighty God. The sheer power and force of those waters cascading over and down, with such an awesome strength, began with one drop of water somewhere.

If we as one-drop Christians join with other one-drop Christians, united we become the awesome power of a Niagara Falls. God can use each and every one of us as He wills. The Bible does tell us that God also will use His church. It's a wonderful blessing to be a child of God, but to be a part of His church is indeed more awesome.

He pools us as those drops of water. We may be dripping slowly over into others' lives to make a difference, or we may be rushing down a river and over the falls to power a whole movement. Only God knows His whole intent for each of our lives, but I do know that as long as we continue to drink from His living waters, our one-drop at a time is of great value to the one living God.

55

Our Alabaster Jar

"Now while Jesus was at Bethany in the house of Simon the leper, a woman came to Him with an alabaster jar of very costly ointment, and she poured it on his head as He sat at the table" (Matthew 26:6-7).

"While He was at Bethany in the house of Simon the leper, as He sat at the table, a woman came with an alabaster jar of very costly ointment of nard, and she broke open; the jar and poured the ointment on His head" (Mark 14:3).

This beautiful story about the woman with the costly alabaster jar of ointment has always been a favorite of mine. She anointed Jesus' body for the burial before He was ever falsely accused, tried, or wickedly crucified, dead, and buried. She performed a ritual that was usually done to a body after death and was being prepared for burial. I've always reveled that she had such insight to have known what Jesus had been telling His disciples all along, though they simply didn't get it.

The story goes that they were angry at her flagrant waste of such an expensive nard. They fumed and fussed about her waste of its precious contents that could have been sold and the money used to help the poor. They scolded her and were caught up in a debate with Jesus over her seemingly thoughtless actions. I feel sure that a woman in those days had no cultural right to defend her actions in a world ruled by and run by men.

Jesus was quick to defend this woman, and let the disciples know that what she did would be told in remembrance of her, whenever and wherever the good news was proclaimed. My Bible reference at the bottom of the page concerning this Scripture says that the woman's act won higher praise from Jesus than any other mentioned in the New Testament. The good service that was good and fitting under the circumstances of impending death were the same Greek words that translated good works.

As I reflect this morning, I'm not so sure that the woman had more insight than any of the disciples about Jesus' impending death. Perhaps she was caught up in the moment. Perhaps her overwhelming love for Jesus, the Messiah, took precedence over anything else. I feel sure that she knew the value of her alabaster jar. An imported jar of nard wasn't something that she had picked up at the corner market.

Just perhaps, she wanted to give to the King of Kings her very best. With no thought of what other worthy and wonderful things the alabaster jar could have been used for, she simply wanted to present it to her Lord and Master. Her love for Jesus empowered the contents of that alabaster jar, far beyond anything that man could have thought of for its purpose. A God of provision had filled her heart so full of love for His only Son that God prepared Jesus' body for burial through this woman.

We too can present Him with our alabaster jars of priceless love, gifts, talents, and blessings. We can lay them at His feet, simply because we love Him and want to give Him our very best. We need not scheme or plan on how to do good service or good works. In love and adoration of Jesus, allow Him to anoint and use the contents of our alabaster jars to glorify His Name.

His divine purpose for each of our lives is fulfilled whenever we present Him with the contents of our alabaster jars. Break open the seal that has held the priceless contents today and pour it out upon the head of Jesus or Lord. Bathe his body with all the love that you feel for Him and allow Him to work in your life as never before. The God of provision can use your gifts and talents today to fulfill His kingdom. The God whose name is synonymous with love asks that we love his Son of love, with all the love that we have, even the contents of our alabaster jars.

56

The Path

"You show me the path of life. In Your Presence there is fullness of joy; in Your right hand are pleasures forevermore" (Psalm 16:11).

I have several pieces of artwork by my son. He's been given a precious gift from God to draw, paint, and sketch such beautiful pieces of art. Not everyone has such a gift, and he is truly blessed to be able to look at anything and put his impressions down on paper or canvas. As a small child he discovered his gift. He was able to look at something with pencil in hand and replicate it without ever looking down at his paper. It was amazing to be able to watch him at such a young age as he sketched his uncle, the UNC Tarheel Ram, or the old feed barn. Whatever his subject, his talent always showed through.

I have one of his sketches of the old feed barn framed in my granddaughter's bedroom. Years ago, I had it framed with remnants from an antique tobacco stick from the same farm. My thoughts were that someday, the framed picture would have a special meaning for him. I'm forever preparing memorabilia for my children to appreciate one day. I have things from the past that I simply enjoy holding, cherishing and walking down memory lane with ever so often. Nostalgia is good thing to be savored and enjoyed occasionally.

As I look at the sketch of the barn, a new appreciation of the artwork catches my eye. My son has sketched or drawn the old barn numerous times, but to my recollection, it's always from the viewpoint that he had as a child. His perspective of the barn is always at the end of the path that led from our house. The end with the tree line, the shed for the tractor, and none of the huge barn doors is always the barn he draws. I think of the many ways that the barn could be depicted. Uncle John would have always come from the other direction and had a different viewpoint. Grandma and Grandpa would have come from the rear and seen a different slant on the old feed barn. Uncle Norman coming up in the front would have had the full countenance of the barn's character. It's as though my son's perspective is forever burned into his artistic eye. His idea of the barn is at the end of that aforementioned path.

Were our lives likened to that old barn, and all of us the artist attempting to render its image for posterity, we would need to sketch each and every aspect in order to get a quality piece of artwork. The whole picture of life isn't just one path or one viewpoint. The whole picture of life is every individual's perspective in a collection of sketches and paths. Jesus gives us that capability when we love each and every soul with the love of Christ. No matter what the path, what the viewpoint, what the differences in thinking might be, we can still all embrace a view of life the way it should be depicted. There are many paths leading to the direction of God. Jesus tells us from His own lips that He is the way. Be assured that when Jesus is the path we take, we will reach our fullness of joy in our relationship with God the Father and get the whole picture.

57

Patriotic Pumpkin

"We know that all things work together for good for those who love God, who are called according to this purpose" (Romans 8:28).

"For we are what He made us, created in Christ Jesus for good works, which God prepared beforehand to be our way of life" (Ephesians 2:10).

"Are you creative? Can you paint?" asked my granddaughter's third grade teacher, as she brought the pumpkin over to my table. I had spent the year volunteering for her on Wednesdays, and was very comfortable being her right-hand woman for any project she might come up with for the class.

Visions of those beautifully painted pumpkins with prize ribbons on them came to my mind. Many times I had enjoyed the artwork at local and state fairs. I knew very well that I was not creative or talented enough to paint one of those pumpkins. I also remembered many years ago trying to paint a pumpkin. All the mistakes and frustrations flooded my mind. My gifts and talents definitely did not include painting.

"Not really," was my reply. "I'll be glad to help you any way you like, though." She quickly began sharing her ideas of an Uncle Sam pumpkin. Since this was a presidential election year and we were so close to the November elections, she thought this an appropriate theme. Each classroom had been assigned to decorate a pumpkin for the school-wide contest. She had this wonderful idea and things simply seemed to come together after that.

At home, I went through my craft cabinets in the basement and collected anything that even remotely looked patriotic. The next morning, our decorations consisted of a red, white and blue basketball net, iron on stars, striped ribbon, and red yarn for hair. Assembly morning, the creative juices flowed. We were all well pleased with our patriotic pumpkin results.

Later that night, I returned from the state fair to an excited message on my answer machine. The teacher had called and was ecstatic about winning first place in the contest. She relayed that the class members were unable to hear what their prize would be because in their excitement they were yelling and clapping. She thanked me again for my help in decorating the pumpkin.

I had already realized that there was a divine hand involved in this endeavor. The supplies that I had bought long ago were exactly the things that pulled everything together. I had no foresight as to how I would ever use them. There were on sale and I remember thinking that they might come in handy one day. The basketball net purchased for one dollar seemed useless because we didn't even have a basketball net. Strange?

Not so strange at all! I know from other experiences in my life that this is exactly how God operates. He has the foresight and the knowledge to pull everything together. All things work together for good for those who love God. In my mind all things would include decorating a pumpkin to make twenty-four little children as happy as this third grade classroom was last Friday afternoon. When God prepares beforehand, He takes all things into consideration and knows exactly what we will need.

It may sound strange to some, but I'm not at all surprised that the loving God we serve isn't too busy or too austere to be involved in something as simple as a pumpkin-decorating contest. Thank you, Lord, for Your guidance and Your all-knowing foresight. Especially thank You for the ability to see Your presence in all things, large and small.

58

Perfect Christmas

"Then suddenly there appeared a host of angels saying, 'Glory to God in the highest and on earth peace, goodwill toward men'" (Luke 2:13-14).

As I sit this morning reflecting on Christmas, that is only seven days away, and marveling at the fact that the older I get, the faster they come and go, I'm struck by that nagging "perfect Christmas" feeling again. I have it annually whenever I reflect on the celebrations of days gone by. I still wait for that perfect Christmas that's filled with cheer, peace, and love abounding.

That perfect Christmas will have all my loved ones gathered in happy celebration of the birth of our Lord and Savior. That perfect Christmas will have friends and family with faces shining with the joy of Christmas, and not one tear will fall for loved ones that have separated from each other or gone on. That perfect Christmas seems only to be an illusion that somehow never seems to materialize because the computer crashed, someone's mad at someone, or the hustle and bustle are just too much! Or, has that perfect Christmas already been?

That perfect Christmas came when God chose to send Himself, his love, and His Son into this world. That perfect Christmas came over two thousand years ago and took place in a lowly manger, not quite my ideal location for perfection to manifest, but God's choice, nonetheless. That perfect Christmas began with pain, as Mary's labor brought forth that bundle of love, grace, and mercy that would touch each of our lives with perfection. It continued in adversity as Mary and Joseph scurried through the crowded streets of Bethlehem to find a safe harbor for Emmanuel to arrive. I can only imagine Mary's frustrations and anxieties as labor quickened and there was nowhere to lay her head for the delivery.

That perfect Christmas was celebrated in a dark and dank stable with the smells of sweat, animals, and hay. There wasn't any cinnamon or cider simmering on the stove, or freshly baked pies in the oven. There were no Christmas carols echoing from the parlor piano. There were no presents under a finely decorated tree. There were no stockings hung by the chimney with care. There were only the odious smells of a world decayed, putrid in the nostrils of God. With animals lowing in a dimly lit stable, God sent that perfect Christmas that would never be surpassed. Our loving God, in His infinite grace, sent Himself manifested in a tiny baby called Jesus.

He sent the way, the truth, and the life into the world so that you and I would be able to celebrate not just the perfect Christmas, but that we might celebrate Him and all His glory for all eternity. He made Himself flesh so that He might live and teach the gospel or good news to each of us. He manifested Himself so that He might suffer and die for all our sins and then He arose so that we might have life eternal. Wow! Such a perfect Christmas and it's ours, yours and mine to celebrate with all of heaven.

As the Babe lay in that darkened manger scene, God brought forth the shepherds from the hillsides. He brought forth wisemen from afar. He brought forth a heavenly choir that has not, nor ever will be, rivaled in all of history. God created the perfect Christmas for us and, by example, showed us what the season is about. We celebrate Jesus' birth with all the holiday trimmings, but do we cast abroad that LOVE that was the whole essence of that perfect Christmas so long ago?

Grab hold of that perfection, my brothers and sisters! Open that perfect gift and allow God to shower your Christmas with the perfection that only He can give. Jesus, manifested and made real in our lives, is the only way to celebrate this day and all days for eternity. "Then suddenly there appeared a host of angels saying, 'Glory to God in the highest and on earth peace, goodwill toward men'" (Luke 2:13-14). Have a merry and perfect Christmas this year by allowing Jesus the Christ into your heart!

59

The Persimmon Tree

"They are like trees planted by streams of water, which yield their fruit in its season, and their leaves do not wither. In all that they do, they prosper" (Psalms 1:3).

The leaves aren't the bright oranges and yellows and reds of the maples that so adorn the autumn landscape every year. The persimmon tree in my back yard has leaves of a persimmon color, umber, soft orange, mellow browns, and burnt sienna. It just so happens on this cloudy day, which has the promise of a long needed rain, that the persimmon tree radiates the soft song of its colors. Its leaves seem to brighten the gray sky and the dried foliage that surrounds it.

I'm amazed that the tree has any color at all after this year of unprecedented drought. This lone persimmon tree in my backyard heralds the changing of the season to all the lifeless grass, shrubbery, and trees around it. The persimmon tree beside it has no leaves and shows signs that it may have died during this drought. The lawn is brown, many plants have long ago lost their leaves for lack of water, and many have died this dry and rainless season.

The thought strikes me that just maybe this persimmon tree has latched onto some underground spring that we've been told runs through the backside of our property. Just beyond the lawn is a wooded area with gullies, creeks, and natural springs. Does the persimmon tree have a long taproot like so many trees have? I don't know. I do know that this lone tree is the only sign of autumn in my backyard that is usually ablaze with the colors of the season.

The thought of our lives and how the conditions around our lives sometimes aren't conducive to our spiritual growth crowds my mind. Life happens to all of us. Age comes; sickness and death touch each of lives. Busyness and the mundane things creep into each day. We often crowd out our time spent with God for necessary things that life requires from each of us. The droughts of life experiences are lethal if we're not tapped into something far deeper and far richer than our life condition.

Our heavenly position is far greater than our earthly condition. Paul prays that, "...according to the riches of His glory, He may grant that we be strengthened in our inner being with power through His Spirit, and that Christ may dwell in our hearts through faith, as we are being rooted and grounded in love" (Ephesians 3:16-17). He continues with this beautiful blessing, "I pray that you may have the power to comprehend, with all the saints, what is the breadth and length and height and depth, and to know the love of Christ that surpasses knowledge, so that you may be filled with all the fullness of God" (Ephesians 3:18-20).

Years ago I remember praying for that fullness of God that Paul describes in these verses. No matter what is going on around us, that fullness will sustain us and keep us grounded in His love. No matter the condition, our position is firm. Firm and on that rock that shall not be moved. His river of living waters, which is His Word to us and in us, shall sustain us and keep us from withering away and succumbing to that life condition around each of our lives.

Get alone with God today and let His word fill you to overflowing. Let His precious word sustain you and equip you for this day and all that is in store for you. Grow in His love, His grace, and His mercy. Allow Him to supply that daily bread and living water that will keep you from withering up and being overcome by all that is around you. Drought is drought, but God is bigger than any drought that may come into our lives. Allow Him to ground you and fill you with His fullness today, and your colors will light up the world around you like that persimmon tree in my back yard. May God fill you to overflowing today with His fullness, and may you prosper in all that you do.

60

Plain Sight

"How beautiful upon the mountains are the feet of the messenger who announces peace, who brings good news, who announces salvation, who says to Zion, 'Your God reigns.' Listen! Your sentinels lift up their voices, together they sing for joy; for in plain sight they see the return of the LORD to Zion. Break forth together into singing, you ruins of Jerusalem; for the LORD has comforted His people, He has redeemed Jerusalem. The LORD has bared His holy arm before the eyes of all the nations; and all the ends of the earth shall see the salvation of our God" (Isaiah 52:7-10).

God does have many plans to keep us in His presence and seeking His holy face. We learn on a need to know basis. Whenever we need to know something in order to deal with it, God in His infinite grace and mercy sends His Holy Spirit with the answer that will get us through that particular valley. Our mandate, then, is to share that particular insight on that mountain top period of our journey. When we've sufficiently witnessed to God's glory, down we must go into that next mysterious valley of need. On and on, we go up and down this journey of life, growing in our relationship with God the whole way.

The Scripture above speaks to my heart about those mountaintop experiences. We must sing to the top of our lungs of the One who brought us through that valley just the other side of the mountaintop. We must share our good news, or the gospel according to us, of how God intersected with our life circumstance. Whenever we're faced with trials, tragedies, disease, or simply life in general, the world is looking at the children of God to see how they might handle just such a crisis in their own life. They, too, are searching for the answers and the Giver of those answers. We must shout to them that our God is real and indeed, in control of all things.

Jesus is the true Son of God. He died and arose from the dead that we might be able to sing of salvation. He sent his Comforter to enable us to face and understand our valley experiences. He was crucified on top of a hill called Golgotha, in plain sight of every passerby on the road into that holy city, Jerusalem. He was in plain sight for those who mourned Him and for those who spat upon Him. He remains in plain sight today for those who seek Him. We need only to use those eyes that the Holy Spirit will endeavor to give us in order to see the resurrected Christ.

He's in plain sight whenever we see the first daffodil of spring shouting of the renewal of life that's in the air. He's in plain sight whenever we hug our grandchild close and smile at some child-like statement of truth they just shared. He's in plain sight as we cherish the love of our spouse who's always there to help us in our time of need. He's in plain sight as we look at the news and see people helping people to face one natural disaster after another. He's in plain sight of every human being ever created by a loving God.

I realize this Scripture is foretelling of Jesus' return to Zion, but God is quickening my heart to the fact that Jesus is in plain sight to those who would see Him. Yes, He will return, but, until that appointed day, He's left His Holy Spirit to live in us that we might ever keep Him in plain sight at all times. We are His hands until that glorious day of His return!

If the LORD has comforted you, then comfort someone else. If the LORD has redeemed you, then point someone in need of redemption toward the living Christ that redeems. If God has favored you, then show favor. If a loving God has blessed you, then in turn be a blessing to those whom you meet along the way. Be a sentinel, lift up your voice; sing for joy in plain sight so that others might see His glory, His goodness, and His grace until that day of His return, when all will see Him in plain sight!

61

The Portal

"For this perishable body must put on imperishability and this mortal body must put on immortality. When this perishable body puts on imperishability, and this mortal body puts on immortality, then the saying that is written will be fulfilled: 'Death has been swallowed up in victory. Where, O death is your victory? Where, O death is your sting?' The sting of death is sin, and the power of sin is the law. But thanks be to God, who gives us the victory through our Lord Jesus Christ" (I Corinthians 15:53-57).

"Where, O death, is your victory? Where, O death, is your sting?" (I Corinthians 15:55) were Biblical phrases that I was exposed to early on in life. I first remember reading them in my high school annual. What prophetic and deep meanings were in those words! At that tender age, I had no real concept of their meaning but I remember thinking they were beautiful words and worth logging into my memory bank. I really don't remember now whether or not I knew that they were from the Bible. I simply thought that they were philosophical and I was about to embark into life with all the eagerness and mentality with which most teenagers are equipped. Most youth think they have the market on wisdom and life, life, life. Death is something so far from their futures that it doesn't warrant much, if any, consideration.

As we age, death still takes a back burner to PTA, soccer games, circle meetings, and life in general. Vacations revitalize, schedules are busy, and no young adult has much time to ponder the complexities of death. Parenting and careers take most of our attention and energy. Sunday school and Bible studies mature our spiritual lives and bring us into a closer relationship to God. Still, most of us are prone to putting off morbid thoughts of old age, reflective years, and death. Those are things we will ponder in our later years.

Before my later years came, a life-threatening disease forced me to face my mortality. I finally realized that we all face death no matter what age, young or old. We all face death each day! We are promised only today. I am so grateful to a God who sent His son Jesus to give us all victory over death. I jokingly have said through the years that it wasn't death I feared, but the dying process! When faced with the real possibility of death, I found I had been lying to myself. I was fearful of death itself, as we all are to some extent. God led me through that valley of the shadow of death, and helped me realize that death isn't a permanent condition. Death is merely a portal through which we all must walk. A shadow, if you will, that He will guide and lead us through.

I write this today because I have dear friends who are standing at that portal. Standing, as I would, with weak knees knocking at the thought of going through that fearsome door. God is letting me know today that portal is simply a door that takes us out of a life of distraction. We spend our whole lives trying to come back into focus on the one true meaning of life, which is a living relationship with God. Our other relationships with family and friends are fruits of our relationship with Him. Throughout life we are distracted by life in general. Once we walk through that portal we are able to leave all those distractions behind. The distraction of pain, the distraction of temptation, the distraction of sin, the distraction of heartache and the distraction of heavy burdens are all left in the room we know as life.

As we walk through that portal into the presence of God, we are at last where we've always longed to be. We are at last through the journey of life and multiple distractions. We are able to focus on the one thing we were created for. We will walk through that portal and be, at last, at peace, the peace that will indeed surpass all our understanding, the peace of life eternal with the one true God. We can take heart and be as brave as our humanity will allow us. We can be of good cheer because God has promised throughout His Holy Word to walk us through that portal. We as Christians can help each other by holding our brother or sister's hand, until the loving Father reaches for their hand to guide them through life's final door. There is no doubt in my mind that He will bring a heavenly host with Him to relieve all our fears and safeguard each passing. Where, O death is your victory? Where, O death is your sting? Our victory in Jesus the Christ has taken that sting of death and put it to rest. Praise God!

62

The Power

"For this reason, I bow my knees before the Father, from whom every family in heaven and on earth takes its name. I pray that, according to the riches of His glory, He may grant that you may be strengthened in your inner being with power through His Spirit, and that Christ may dwell in your hearts through faith, as you are being rooted and grounded in love. I pray that you may have the power to comprehend, with all the saints, what is the breadth and length and height and depth, and to know the love of Christ that surpasses knowledge, so that you may be filled with all the fullness of God. Now to Him who by the power at work within us is able to accomplish abundantly far more than all we can ask or imagine, to Him be glory in the church and in Christ Jesus to all generations, forever and ever. Amen" (Ephesians 3:14-21).

I awake at 7:15 today. The Russians are coming! I've been preparing for their visit for nearly two weeks now. A group of touring Russian singers is to sing at an area church on Friday night, and we are fortunate enough to be hosting two of them. I've been cleaning and shining in anticipation of their arrival. I've been so very excited about this opportunity for cultural exchange and can't wait to be blessed by their visit.

Finally, the day has arrived! As I rise from bed, I quickly make it. In my mind I run over all the last minute things I need to do before I pick them up at 3:00 this afternoon. From the bedroom I go to the kitchen to make my morning coffee. Just as I reach for the pot, it happened. The power went out. Oh no! Not today! What could it be?

A quick check let me know it was out everywhere. I kept my cool and did all the things I could without power and especially without my morning coffee. I thought, I'd go ahead and do my devotional and "get it out of the way." No power needed in that endeavor. I quickly read my Bible verses, upper room, and prayed my prayers. Still, there was no power.

As I sat there on the couch thinking of all the things I needed power in order to do, such as the dryer for one last load of clothes, the hair dryer after shampooing my hair, and the oven to make the dessert I had planned to bake this morning, I felt powerless. What can I do? Then the memory of last Tuesday night came to me.

In our lay speaking class we had to deliver a five-minute sermon. I remembered one of my new friend's sermons had been about plugging into God's power. As I went to my notebook to find the Bible text she had used, the power came on. What an affirmation that was to me. God had wanted me to start my day and this encounter with strangers plugged into His power. As I read this text, I noticed the highlighting and the note I had written earlier in the margin, a beautiful blessing.

I've read these verses before many times, and never thought about this text plugging me into God's power. Thank you, God, for little inconveniences and spiritual bumpers that guide us into the path You want for us. I'm thankful for the living Word that God guided me to today and am ready to be abundantly blessed for the rest of this beautiful day. God's power is on and I'm definitely plugged in.

63

Real Rock

"…not everyone who says to me 'Lord, Lord,' will enter the kingdom of heaven…" (Matthew 7:21-27).

These Scriptures, and especially the one quoted above, strike an unwarranted fear in me. I'm a believer. I'm a child of God. I feel I'm in God's will for me, but this passage tells me I can be all these things and still miss the mark. Recently, God showed me an example of how easy missing the mark might be.

Yesterday, we bought some more edging to put around the pool area. I have discovered this beautiful plastic edging that looks exactly like rock. Instead of being heavy, burdensome, and hard to work with, it's very user friendly. Once placed in the ground, it would be hard for someone else to see that it isn't really rock. Though the appearance of this edging looks like the real thing, it definitely won't be around one hundred years from now like a natural rock would be. It's a quick fix. We must be leery in our spiritual lives of quick fixes.

The real thing, the real rock, the one true God, will be around for all eternity. We must not miss the mark and live only a user friendly, imitation of the one life on earth that He's given us. We must chisel, sweat under the burden, and get our hands dirty building our spiritual houses on the real rock. In other words, we must participate in life. We must be the physical hands of God in the mission fields. We must be out on the street and in the places we may go, declaring that Jesus is Lord of our lives. We can't simply attend church once a week and not live the Christian life the other six days. That would be like the plastic edging that I spoke of earlier. We need to let every encounter we have during each day be hands on experience for God.

To think that going to church and being a good person is enough to get us into heaven may just cause us to miss the mark. A spiritual life that is rooted and grounded in the real rock, Jesus Christ, will bear fruit. These passages tell us that a wise man builds his house on the rock...Living and working with real rock isn't always user friendly. Indeed, when that great day of judgment comes, we can feel assured that He will know us by the sweat on our brows and the calluses on our hands.

64

Recognize Him

"Trust in the LORD with all your heart, and do not rely on your own insight. In all your ways acknowledge Him, and He will make straight your paths. Do not be wise in your own eyes; fear the LORD, and turn away from evil. It will be a healing for your flesh and a refreshment for your body" (Proverbs 3:5-8).

I can always remember a love for cloud watching. As a small child, I recall many a warm summer day spent daydreaming, and watching those billowy clouds change from one recognizable thing into another. Yesterday, my grandson and I spent a few restful minutes trying to label and decide what this cloud or that cloud looked like to us. He would get excited about a dragon or whatever else he thought he saw and be very impatient with me, until I could finally come into agreement with him on his imaginary discovery.

My gaze turns heavenward this morning during my meditation time, and I can see divine inspiration in those same cottony, white and random puffs. The morning sky is full of wisps and swirls going in all directions and then, from nowhere, there seems to be a straight brush-like stroke painted right through the midst of them all. I'm reminded that God turned chaos into divine order. I'm reminded that in the middle of whatever is going on in our lives each day, God is indeed present and running right through the middle of every confusing or hectic wisp or swirl that we might encounter.

Sometimes we are much like those random clouds, floating around, bumping into this or that. We're constantly changing from this mood or that emotion. It's easy to be buffeted around and fall prey to disorder, chaos, and yes evil. We must be alert and keep our eyes open to see that God of divine order throughout our day. For eyes that see, He can be found over, under, and throughout every moment of every day. For eyes that can't see, extra effort should be made to find that straight and constant brush stroke that is intermingled with all those other things that confront us daily.

This Scripture reminds us to trust the LORD and not be as my little grandson, and get impatient or rely on our own insight about what's going on around us. Once we recognize that God is in it and taking care of us to make our path straight, we are indeed refreshed and healed from an array of things. We must be quick to come into agreement with the fact that God is that one faithful and steadfast thing that will guide us through this life. Acknowledge Him in all things and He will be that healing and refreshing balm so sorely needed for our hurting lives. Praise Him, glorify Him, and most certainly recognize Him throughout each and every busy moment of your day.

Psalm 121 is one of the most encouraging Psalms written. It promises security and freedom from any wispy, billowy thing that might arise in our lives. "I lift up my eyes to the hills—from where will my help come? My help comes from the LORD, who made heaven and earth. He will not let your foot be moved...The LORD is your keeper; He who keeps you will not slumber or sleep...The sun shall not strike you by day, nor the moon by night...The LORD will keep you from all evil; He will keep your life. The LORD will keep your going out and your coming in from this time forevermore" (Psalms 121:1-8).

You can't get much plainer, straighter, or recognizable than those words in Psalm 121. He's there in the midst of it all and handling it for us. He's there protecting, guiding, and leading us. Begin by making a conscious effort to recognize Him in even the smallest of things and before long, you'll find that you don't have to make any effort at all. You'll easily see Him over, under and throughout. Recognize Him, trust Him, thank Him, and most of all, praise Him.

65

Red Hat Dancing

"You have turned my mourning into dancing; You have taken off my sackcloth and clothed me with joy, so that my soul may praise You and not be silent. O LORD my God, I will give thanks to You forever" (Psalms 30:11-12).

As a woman of strong faith and blessings too numerous to list, I must admit that when I lost three grandchildren in a senseless automobile accident, I was brought to my knees and journeyed through a land that was foreign to me. That place where I visited on a daily basis was the land of grief.

Although God was with me through the whole tragedy, I still would slip into doubt, self-pity, and a sadness of spirit that gripped me with a death hold, as wrestlers would say. My cheerful, happy demeanor became what I now refer to as my Jobetta (Book of Job) Year. I knew without a doubt that I couldn't allow this event to define my life as a Christian, wife, mother, and grandmother. I knew without a doubt that I should not linger in this land of grief a day longer than necessary, or I might never find my way out.

Many things led to my journey back to life after the accident. My husband, my church, numerous friends and family members were there to love me and try their best to help me through a hurt so deep. I know for a fact that a broken heart will not kill you but make you stronger. I had to get alone with God and allow Him to heal me. I found myself alone more and more as the days, weeks, and months went by. I found myself cradled in His divine arms. I sat on His precious lap and allowed Him to stroke my brow and let me know that things would be all right.

The God we serve is faithful to supply all our needs and He showed me through a year of brokenness and mourning that He is faithful to heal all our hurts. He is faithful to supply exactly what we need on a moment by moment basis. Just the right card arriving in the mail, a phone call when we need it most, a hug from someone next to us in our pew, or whatever we might need to catch a glimpse of Him in our day of sorrow, He is faithful to supply.

Now I'd like to give you my "red hat testimony," as I call it. About a year after the accident, I came across the above Scripture during my daily Bible reading and devotional time. It was like flashing lights, whistles and bells went off in my head! God spoke to me, not in an audible voice, but through every fiber of my being, and let me know that it was time to laugh. Yes, laugh is the word I heard as clearly as if someone had spoken it in my ear.

God gifted me with a cheerful personality and it had been buried for nearly a year in the deep and dark pits of grief and sadness beyond anything I had ever experienced. Now, out of the blue, He was saying, laugh. I know the Bible tells us that laughter does the body good, like a medicine, but laughter isn't something that we can produce spontaneously, simply because we will it.

As I sat there and meditated on the verse, the thoughts of being able to laugh again appealed to my spirit. Laughter…laughter…laughter! As I continued to contemplate laughter, a smile grabbed hold of the corner of my mouth, as I remembered the Easter parade the year before, and that gorgeous red hat float that had caught my eye and tweaked my curiosity.

I immediately put down my Bible and went to the computer to do a Google search on the Red Hat Society. That site gave me more information than my hormonally challenged brain could absorb. Page after page of new and exciting things to do met my gaze. Fun things to do! Laughter…laughter…laughter! God let me know that it was time to take off my sackcloth and clothe myself with joy and laughter.

To make a long story short, I searched and found a chapter in my area, and initially joined a group from a neighboring town. I went out with them a time or two and enjoyed myself immensely. I was laughing again, and it felt good. Although I didn't know a one of the members before that first outing, they were kind, funny, and allowed me to join in just like I had always been one of them.

I later decided to start my own chapter with friends from church. Although I didn't want to be "Queen Mum," I decided to be "The Grand Duchess of Writeth Muchus," as God has gifted me with writing devotions through the years. I positioned myself as the chapter's "Exalted Girl Friday," or secretary, social co-coordinator, and any other "unofficial" title that I might later think to call myself.

This all took place years ago, and The Royal Sisterhood of Rowdy Red Hatters was formed and continues to thrive in rural North Carolina. Our membership hovers around thirty. Once a month we have a Fabulous Friday Flop Night at my house with different themes and menus. We've had luaus, banana split suppers, baked potato night, anything that is fun and stress-free. We kick back and watch wonderful movies together and have lots of girl time.

Of course, we go out once a month in full regalia too. We've sailed the Catawba Queen and been to fancy tea rooms for exquisite cuisine. We've toured wineries and often enjoy live theater in a nearby city. We've done many things through the years but the most important thing we've done is laugh...laugh... laugh! The Red Hat Society has been my source of laughter for years now, and I thank God that He led me to the above Scripture and the Red Hat Society. God can turn our mourning into dancing!

66

The Right Time and the Right Direction

"For everything there is a season, and a time for every matter under heaven; a time to be born, and a time to die...a time to love, and a time to hate; a time for war, and a time for peace...I know that whatever God does endures forever; nothing can be added to it, nor anything taken from it; God has done this, so that all should stand in awe before Him. That which is, already has been; that which is to be, already is; and God seeks out what has gone by" (Ecclesiastes 3:1-8, 14-15).

As I finish my Sunday school lesson reading this evening just at dusk, I look up into the sky at the exact moment that three different planes are criss-crossing overhead. One is flying toward the East, one toward the West and one is headed straight Northwest. I have to catch my breath at the wonder of it all. How in the world can they intersect at the same point and the same time, oblivious to each other? Of course, I know they are flying at different altitudes, but it's still an amazing sight that quickens my heart and makes me marvel at man and technology.

The lesson pointed out that our clock time (chronos) and God's fullness of time (kairos) were not the same time. God's time of truth and love and justice and peace doesn't adhere to the chronological ticking of our clocks, the author says. God's fullness of time always allows things to happen at the "right" time, no matter the hour on our wristwatches or wall clocks. We've all experienced this in our prayer lives, and know that God will act in His time and that His timing is impeccable.

My mind is racing at the parallel between time and direction. We Christians all can easily sense the time or season that we're in today. Without claiming to be prophets of doom, we can see the Biblical prophecies and Scriptures being fulfilled right and left. There aren't many Christians around that won't readily agree we're quite possibly in the last days. Or are we?

I can say with all assuredness that these are your last days. These are without a doubt my last days. This is why every generation has had that eerie premonition of being in the last days. Our chronos calendars are sure indicators of our limited time and our last day awareness. But God's kairos, right time, puts us on a completely different altitude or line of travel.

His fullness of time overrides our chronos time so that we might be oblivious to the natural forces of nature and aging. Einstein's theory that time is relative can be illustrated any morning we head off to work or to an appointment. If we leave early, time is ample and we have time to kill. If we leave late, time flies and there isn't nearly enough of it. Time is relative to what we are doing or our attitude/altitude of sensitivity to it.

"God has done this, so that all should stand in awe before Him. That which is, already has been; that which is to be, already is; and God seeks out what has gone by" (Ecclesiastes 3:14-15). Just maybe God is seeking that time in the garden, when man was in complete obedience and fellowshipped with Him on a daily basis. Just maybe God is yearning for that time when all of His creation was traveling in the same direction, an eternity of love, obedience, and relationship with the Creator. Just maybe God's fullness of time is hinging on our willingness to travel at the right altitude going in the right direction.

Our Bibles tells us the direction and the Way. The Way has a name, and His Name is Jesus. His willingness to cross over the kairos time of eternity into our chronos times to live and die for our sins is sure proof of God's willingness and desire to seek us out. He gave His all that we might change our direction and live in His fullness or kairos time. "For everything there is a season," (Ecclesiases 3:1) and my spirit tells me that this is the season and the right time to go in the right direction. Stand in awe before Him the Creator of time, both chronos and kairos!

67

The Right Voice

"Very truly, I tell you, anyone who does not enter the sheepfold by the gate but climbs in by another way is a thief and a bandit. The one who enters by the gate is the shepherd of the sheep. The gatekeeper opens the gate for him, and the sheep hear his voice. He calls his own sheep by name and leads them out. When he has brought out all his own, he goes ahead of them, and the sheep follow him because they know his voice. They will not follow a stranger, but they will run from him because they do not know the voice of strangers. Jesus used this figure of speech with them, but they did not understand what he was saying to them. So again Jesus said to them, 'Very truly, I tell you, I am the gate for the sheep. All who came before me are thieves and bandits; but the sheep did not listen to them. I am the gate. Whoever enters by me will be saved, and will come in and go out and find pasture. The thief comes only to steal and kill and destroy, I came that they may have life, and have it abundantly'" (John 10:1-10).

We all are products of events and people who enter, stay a while, and leave our lives. The Bible tells us that there is nothing new under the sun. Our characters and personalities are products of a culmination of things that we've seen, read, heard, or experienced throughout our lifetime. I am in awe of young folks who find Jesus at an early age and are listening to the right voice throughout most of their lives here on Earth. I'm one of those later bloomers who never tuned in to that right voice until my midyears. I'm one of those who regrets wasted years and lost opportunities for the Lord. I try not to dwell on them but there are still times that I visit there.

A recent email about contemporary Christian music unsettled me. I thought that I had a handle on how I felt about this issue. I thought surely Jesus would use this format, were He here today, to reach teens on a level that would speak to them. I personally love those "seven eleven songs," as I've heard them called. Seven words sung eleven times brings home a good message and praise time that is so much easier for an older person like me who misses their memory.

As I reflect on the other side of this issue, I'm not sure I do have a handle on it. God's message never changes. He tells us that He's the same yesterday, today, and forever. The message is attractive in and of itself. Why should anyone have to adapt it to suit anything? Pretty packaging or a modern slant on the ageless truth could, I guess, be misconstrued as climbing in another way and not through the gate. I think, though, it's the packaging and not the message that has been changed.

Could a whole generation and many clergy be wrong about this issue? Could contemporary Christian music be a vehicle to water down or change the importance and truth of the gospel? It's a valid question that we face today, and I most certainly don't have the answer. I'm still undecided as to how I feel, myself. I do know that we are not to be of this world. We are called to be a peculiar people and be set apart from this world. That's a plus for the anti- "contemporary Christian music" side, but then again, I know that Jesus was radical when He walked this Earth and did things in a new and different way that the established church of His day frowned upon.

Maybe we should leave the final decision to each person and God. The Bible tells us that, "All things work together for good for those who love God, who are called according to His purpose" (Romans 8:28). It also says, "Now the Lord is the Spirit, and where the Spirit of the Lord is, there is freedom" (II Corinthians 3:17). Psalms tells us, "Praise the LORD! Sing to the LORD a new song, His praise in the assembly of the faithful...Let them praise His name with dancing, making melody to Him with tambourine and lyre. For the LORD takes pleasure in his people" (Psalms 149:1-4).

We all should judge not, lest we be judged, and allow the freedom that the Spirit of the Lord affords each of His children. As long as we are listening to the Good Shepherd whose own sheep know His voice, we are listening to the right voice. Jesus told us, "In my Father's house are many mansions, and I go there to prepare a place for you" (John 14:2). If we Christians are each to have a mansion or room in our Father's house, it's going to be a pretty large place. Something is assuring me that not every one of those mansions will be stereotyped. There will be variety. My Father God is so diversified; I cannot begin to comprehend all the differences and assortment that we will find there.

68

The Rose of Sharon

"But this is the covenant that I will make with the house of Israel
after those days, says the LORD: I will put my law within them and
I will write it on their hearts; and I will be their God and they shall
be my people" (Jeremiah 31:33).

Rose of sharon, hibiscus syriacus, isn't a rose, but its large blossoms attract hummingbirds and tiny insects that hummers also eat. The flowers on this woody shrub come in several colors, including white, pink, purple, and red. Its leaves don't come out until late in spring, causing false alarms in gardeners who think their plants may have died.

As I marvel at how many blooms are on my purple rose of sharon this year, I'm taken back to my childhood when I never knew the beautiful, Biblical name of this particular shrub. As a child in the country, we always called them cotton bushes. That's what I was told they were, and that's what I called them until adulthood.

I can remember that there was always an abundance of them wherever we lived or visited. One of my favorite games as a child was playing with the unopened buds of the cotton bush. My imagination turned them into every possible toy. They could be anything from a missile thrown at cousins to some exotic food to prepare in my pretend string playhouse. The different colors made a beautiful array on top of many a mud pie.

As an adult, I was somewhat surprised to learn that the proper name for this very familiar shrub was rose of sharon. How beautiful, I remember thinking. Why in the world would people call it something as ordinary and mundane as a cotton bush, when it could be called something as beautiful sounding and special as rose of sharon? The fact that our Lord Jesus could be described as the Rose of Sharon or Lily of the Valley indeed adds to that special title for such a lovely shrub.

Recently in a conversation with my aunt, we discussed that neither of us could name an exact date and time of our baptism into the Holy Spirit. We are both assured that we are children of the one living God, but we lack that precise credibility that many TV evangelists seem to have when they can quote an exact time, place and date of their salvation. I'm humbled and in awe when I hear a witness from a fellow Christian stating their witness with such accuracy. I've never been able to put a time, place, or date to my walk with God. It's been more of a gradual process. It's been more of a journey that I can always remember being on.

When I told my aunt that I'd always sensed God's presence in my life even as a small child, her comment kind of startled me. "I wonder where you got it from; you surely didn't get it from your Mama or Daddy." Though my childhood lacked a proper church-involved upbringing, God surrounded me with many wonderful opportunities, and people to make me aware of a loving God that was always ever near.

Though the true Rose of Sharon may have come as just a cotton bush, He had written it on my heart to recognize and embrace those large colorful blossoms much like the hummingbird. I recently read in a book about an old saying that in Heaven everyone's cup of joy will be full, but some cups will be larger than others. That is the degree to which we shall be able to see God, and it will depend in part on the perfecting of our spiritual vision here and now. That's an exciting thought!

God is ever near and present in our lives. We must have those spiritual eyes to see Him in all things around us. We must be able to see that the cotton bush is also the beautiful rose of sharon. I praise Him this morning for calling me unto Him, even as a child, before I knew His proper name. Before I could recognize Him as the Great I Am, I knew Him. I've always known Him and am ever grateful for His grace and mercy. Thank you, God, for coming into my heart, first as an ordinary cotton bush, and finally as the beautiful rose of sharon. Thank you for writing Your word on my heart, that I might be a child of the living God.

69

Seek Him First

"But seek ye first the kingdom of God and His righteousness; and all these things shall be added unto you" (Matthew 6:33).

I continue to be amazed at how God uses my kitty cat, Boots of Grace, to speak to me concerning my relationship with Him. Daily, Boots teaches me little life lessons that affirm and reaffirm the word of God that is written in the Bible. Too many times to list, she shows me God's grace abounding in my life, thus her name, Boots of Grace. Repeatedly I've stated that I'm a simple country girl and God makes His message simple for even someone like me.

As I pet and stroke and love on Boots this morning, I'm stricken by her motivation that causes her to seek me out each morning. No matter what, she seeks me first in her day. If I'm allowed to sleep late and am lying in the bed, as my husband lets her up into the house for a little while before he leaves for work, she seeks me out. She's up on the bed, onto my chest, and in my face, seeking her morning loving. Should she still be in the basement when I let her out in the mornings, she's adamant about coming to the door that will gain her access to my lap, whether front door or back door. Should I be on the deck when she starts her day or the front porch, she's in my lap there and wants to be no other place.

Shortly after she's had all the petting, stroking, and loving that she needs, she's off. She's out and about, doing whatever it is that cats do all day. Sometimes I see her daydreaming and plotting at the birdfeeder. Sometimes, she's playing frantically with a grasshopper that gives her the action of play she so desperately desires. Other times, she can be found basking in the sunlight and stretching those legs and head, like only a cat can do. Then there are times she spends the whole day in the woods, doing who knows what. No matter what her day holds, she seeks me out to get her morning loving first and foremost.

As I reflect on that this morning, I realize that I'm the same way. I must seek God early in the morning to have a fulfilling day. It sets the tone for my day. I realize that some folks do this in the evening or all throughout the day. Whatever works is good for them. But, as for me, I must seek Him in the early morning…that's just our designated and appointed time to commune, pray, and just love on each other. Some mornings will vary in the loving. There are days when I need extra love and care and simply crawl up into His lap and feel His love envelop me like the biggest and softest comforter I could find. He surrounds me with His grace, which is indeed sufficient to meet all my needs for that day.

Then there are days when I want to love on Him. I simply want to be in His presence and experience Him for who He is. He is God! He is the Almighty! He is Majesty! He is LORD! He is the Great I Am and He wants to spend His precious and holy time with little old me. I love Him beyond all that I can describe in mere words. I delight in His presence. I hunger after Him like that Psalmist speaks about the deer, panting and thirsting for water. He is my source, my refuge, and my fortress. He is my dearest and closest friend. He is my father, my mother, my sister, my brother, and my husband. He is everything I'll ever need and for that I love Him beyond anything that I can possibly think of or describe.

I guess people are more like the animal world than we might like to admit. I'm so much like Boots, in that each morning I must fill a basic need. That need is to be loved and accepted for who I am. Needing to be loved is one of man's most basic instincts, whether he is willing to admit it or not. Sometimes we throw up that defensive attitude that it doesn't matter, but we're only fooling ourselves. We need to be loved beyond our capacity to love. Only God can fulfill that basic need.

Only God loves us, warts and all. Only God can give us that morning loving that will sustain us through each day. Seek Him out before you're off doing whatever it is you might do each day. Seek Him out before you're out in heavy traffic and off to work. Seek Him out before the school bus runs. Seek Him out before that first doctor's appointment. Seek Him out before that first errand is run to the grocery store or market place. Seek Him out first and foremost because He is already seeking you out. He loves you beyond anything you can ever comprehend or receive. His morning loving is awaiting each of us today. Let's all climb into His lap and receive it. Glory to God for everything He has done.

70

Servant or Slave

"Who among you would say to your slave who has just come in from plowing or tending sheep in the field, 'Come here at once and take your place at the table?' Would you not rather say to him, 'Prepare supper for me, put on your apron and serve me while I eat and drink; later you may eat and drink?' Do you thank the slave for doing what was commanded? So you also, when you have done all that you were ordered to do, say, 'We are worthless slaves; we have done only what we ought to have done'" (Luke 17:7-10)

"Blessed are those slaves whom the master finds alert when He comes; truly I tell you, He will fasten His belt and have them sit down to eat, and He will come and serve them. If He comes during the middle of the night, or near dawn, and finds them so, blessed are those slaves" (Luke 12:37-38).

I began this year with the resolution to do my very best to become a good and faithful servant. Servant is a word used plentifully throughout Scripture. We are servants together. Jesus was a servant to all mankind. Jesus was a servant to the disciples when He humbly washed their feet. Servitude is one of the greatest of all traits and Jesus gave us the ultimate example to follow. A true Christian and follower of Christ knows in his or her heart that serving others is one of the greatest deeds we can possibly do to show our beloved Lord that we love Him.

As I read this morning about rewards and blessings for following the path that Jesus so willfully followed, I'm stricken with query by the use of the two words, servant and slave. For the casual reader, they seem at first glance to be synonymous with each other. We as free men and women have more than likely never considered the fact that there is a difference between these two words. A servant, more than likely, would work for wages or some sort of reward for their services. A slave, on the other hand, doesn't have that luxury. A slave's only reward would be to have his service be a pleasing thing to his master.

We are quick to name Jesus the Christ our Lord and Master, but I seriously doubt that we've truly considered the full meaning of those words. Of course, He asks us to be servants and love one another, as He loves each of us. Therein lies most of our worldly blessings. Yet, today I realize that He asks us to take an even higher step in the direction of His will for our individual lives. He asks us to be slaves, lock, stock, and barrel, as the saying goes. Slaves to the Master afford us no promise of wages or rewards here on Earth. Looking at Jesus' short span of years in this world, I can see that He, Himself, was never rewarded in this life. He was a true slave to the one true God.

As slaves to our risen Lord, we can rest assured that our reward lies in the afterlife. As we each travel our individual journeys with Jesus, we can aspire to love Him enough to become His slave, as well as His servant. His slave would want nothing more than to love Him and please Him. That alone is reward and blessing enough for this slave. We should strive, not only to be good and faithful servants, but to take another step in the direction toward heaven. We should strive to be a slave to the risen Christ. May all that we say and do be pleasing in Your sight, our Lord, our Strength, our Redeemer and yes, our Master. We have done only what we ought to have done. Blessed be the slaves of Jesus our Lord.

71

Shoes that Don't Match

"Pursue peace with everyone, and the holiness without which no one will see the Lord. See to it that no one fails to obtain the grace of God: that no root of bitterness springs up and causes trouble, and through it many become defiled" (Hebrews 12:14-15).

As I look down at my feet, I'm embarrassed for myself to have on mismatched bedroom slippers. "Oh my gosh!" I squealed as I shook my head and went back to the closet to retrieve a matching slipper. I had gone to the closet earlier and slipped them on without looking down. One is brown, one is gray, and they aren't even the same style. I can't for the life of me believe how scattered and senile I'm getting.

I wake up each day and begin my conversation with God as I lie under the covers for a quick snooze session. Like the all too familiar joke, as soon as my feet hit the floor, all my good intentions turn to mush as I deal with getting everyone off for the day. I'm anxious to get everyone out of the house because that's when I can go spend quality time with God. Most mornings there are the usual squabbles about hurrying up to eat breakfast, what to wear for the day, and final instructions on what to do and not do while on the bus and at school.

We've begun saying a prayer of protection for my granddaughter each morning before she faces all the outside influences that children are bombarded with each day. We pray for her to have wisdom to make right choices and clarity of mind to tackle her schoolwork as she deals with attention deficit. Most days she's quick to thank us and says that it does make a difference in how well her day plays out. Her grades this year have proven that prayer does indeed empower her to overcome some obstacles.

When I finally am able to get my Bible and spend my quality time with the Lord, I'm ashamed to admit that more times than not, I feel guilty about how the morning has gone. A lost temper, a nagging bout, or some other carnal fit has taken away any bit of holiness that I might have attained during my earlier snooze sessions while still in bed. I must spend time uprooting seeds of bitterness and pursuing the peace and holiness, without which I can't come into the presence of the Lord. God meets me only after I've purged my heart of the defilement and have repented for my loss of control, hurt feelings or some other discontentment that popped up. His grace is the only thing that can bring me back to the peaceful place where I might fellowship with Him.

Starting the day without God is much like starting the day with shoes that don't match. Things just don't run as smoothly, and for some unexplainable reason we can't get the full grace from God that this Scripture speaks about. God is a God of order and will always enable us to wear shoes that match and fit. He wants us to wear the shoes we need each day to face the outside influences that bombard us each day just as my granddaughter is faced with at school. Those shoes are a part of the whole armor of God that we must put on each day through prayer.

Ephesians 6:15 says, "As shoes for your feet put on whatever will make you ready to proclaim the gospel of peace." Ephesians 6:10-17 is a Scripture that I've put to memory and recite each day during my prayer time. God has let me know today that I must don that armor while still under the covers enjoying my snooze session. Before my feet hit the floor each morning, I must already have on those shoes of peace. They match and they will empower me to face morning squabbles, spilled milk, or any other mishap that might otherwise steal my joy.

Satan is wily enough to know that I'm not tempted to murder or steal or do something blatant to break my relationship with God. He does know me well enough to shoot those flaming arrows that will target my impatience and deep need for everything to run smoothly in the mornings. Those subtle things that rob us of our peace separate us from God, just as readily as those big sins. Sin is sin! There are no big or small ones. Anything that separates us from our relational fellowship with God is sin.

I'll be more prepared tomorrow morning when my feet hit the floor. My shoes will match before I ever put on those slippers, whether they match or not. I intend to suit up with my armor while still under the covers. God's grace never ceases to amaze me and I can never thank Him enough, nor deserve His mercies each day. Be blessed and put on your shoes of peace today! Put them on before your feet hit the floor. Put them on and live in the fullness of God's grace and peace!

72

Sit by the Well and Rest

"...but those who drink of the water that I will give them will never be thirsty. The water that I will give will become in them a spring of water gushing up to eternal life" (John 4:14).

Sit by the well and rest, until all worries and fears fade. Sit by the well and rest until the love of God fills and overflows within you. My backyard pool is my well. There's nothing quite as relaxing and soothing as sitting beside water. Water has a calming effect on a spirit. Just visualizing a pool of water has to make the heart rate go down and summon a calm thought process.

The rippling movement caused by the gentle breeze on my backyard pool catches my eye. The sunlight as it tops the eastern horizon dances on the water and each ripple is a work of art. The patterns cast upon the back wall of the pool look like those squiggly lines of an electric current seen on natural science programs. They glitter and wiggle into such a beautiful pattern, I'm reminded of the white caps of waves as they meet the shoreline. My eyes savor each captivating scenario as the rising sun's rays play with the pool of water.

As we sit by our well and rest, we should give each worry and care that would otherwise weigh us down to God in heaven. Give Him every doubt, every fear. Which direction shall we go today? We give it to You, Lord. How will we deal with this or that? We give it to You, Lord. What about this particular problem or that troublesome person? We give it to You, Lord. On and on we could go as we sit by our well and rest.

As soon as a particular thought or worry comes to mind, give it to Him.

Don't allow anything to creep in and take away more than a fleeting moment before you give it to God. This is your time to sit by the well and rest. It's necessary, and God wants this time for you and me each day, as we walk humbly before our Lord.

As we continue this particular exercise we can feel our load begin to lighten. This must be how God intends for us to begin each and every day. I read somewhere that our spiritual journey is much like a man on a march. There is no need to carry worn out shoes and uniforms from past marches and years. There is no need to carry awkward and bundlesome supplies that we may never need. We need to carry only what we need for that day's march. God will supply all we'll need. If we carry only what we need for today, indeed, our yoke is easy and our burden is light.

I strongly urge anyone to begin his or her day sitting by the well and resting. Cast your cares upon the waters as you sit there in the company of a loving God. We don't need a natural, earthly well. Sit by the wellspring of life. Drink long and hard for the day's journey. Drink from the living Waters until you become that spring of gushing waters. Give Him all your cares. Give Him all your concerns. Give Him all your worries. Rest in Him and He will carry your load.

73

Soar Like the Eagle

"…but those who wait for the LORD shall renew their strength, they shall mount up with wings like eagle's, they shall run and not be weary, they shall walk and not faint" (Isaiah 40:31).

"…who satisfies you with good as long as you live, so that your youth is renewed like the eagle's" (Psalm 103:5).

As I'm lead to Psalm 103 in my devotional this morning, God floods my spirit with this message to write. I need to hear this, someone else needs to hear this, and each of us needs to hear this. God has promise after promise in His precious Word for our good, and we read those promises often times without really thinking about what they might mean literally.

There are many Scriptures referring to eagles and soaring above the earth and although they sound poetic and offer us a sublime thought picture, do we really understand what the writers of God's holy Word are saying? Literally, think of the eagle and what it symbolizes. The strength and agility of an eagle is a role model for all of us . Soaring above the junk going on around us is a goal we should strive for each day.

I received an email some months ago with the plight of the eagle. The eagle lives a very long life. Daily hunting, soaring, and nesting takes a toll on the eagle's body and at the age of thirty, it flies up high to an obscure crevice on a mountaintop and begins to pluck at its own feathers. It pulls and tugs and gets off all the damaged and old feathers, scars, mites, whatever it may be. It bloodies its head, and looks a horribly pitiful sight per the email I read. Then after all this self-purging, it begins to renew. New down feathers and beautiful pinions appear, and the eagle goes out to live another ten or so years with renewed strength, body, and vigor. He's virtually gotten a new lease on life.

Wow! God has promised us that very miraculous process! Can you imagine? At any age we can get rid of all the past sins, the bad memories, the health issues, the stuff that weighs so many of us down, and begin anew. Of course, through Christ, we can become this new creation at any time during our life, but as I age, I love the visual promise that this eagle story provides for our senior years.

We can molt, tug, rebuke, and get rid of anything that might scar us or deter us from being about our Father's business. This Scripture literally says that we can satisfy ourselves with good things and renew our health and youth like the eagles. Good food ingested may just get rid of all the health effects of bad stuff ingested in years past. Forgiveness and love in large doses can undo lots of damage in years past. Self-examination and change through the Holy Spirit is a continual journey in this pilgrimage called life. God will never leave us where He found us! He is constantly changing us into His likeness. God's promises are for all of us, and we can claim them for our lives, knowing that God is faithful and will able to give us all that He has promised.

So, all this being said, get off to yourself and begin the process if you feel you need it. Open God's Word and let Him begin to pick and prod and renew. It may be painful. It may not be a pretty sight, but know that when it's over, God will enable you to soar to new heights. Know that your senior years will be enjoying the "goodness of the LORD in the land of the living" (Psalm 27:13), as promised. Our golden years can be just that, golden!

Instead of looking for healing and rest, enjoy your new energy and become instruments of God's healing to others. Reach out and help someone else today. Statistics say that volunteers live longer lives than folks who sit home and do nothing. Retirement isn't Biblical, brothers and sisters. Stagnation isn't good for anything; just look at how nasty stagnant water can get. God can use your gifts and talents until you draw your last breath on this side of Heaven.

In this newest of years, renew, revive, and reawaken to God's promise for each of us. Get out today and soar like that Biblical eagle. Become all that God has for you, and never miss out because of stuff that can be purged, picked, and discarded, stuff that doesn't matter in the scheme of God's plans for your life. Purge that unnecessary stuff that God can replace with His goodness that does matter here today and for all eternity. Soar, mighty eagle, soar!

74

Sow Seeds

"Hear, O Israel: The Lord is our God, the Lord alone. You shall love the Lord your God with all your heart, and with all your soul and with all your might. Keep these words that I am commanding you today in your heart. Recite them to your children and talk about them when you are at home and when you are away. When you lie down and when you rise. Bind them as a sign on your hand, fix them as an emblem on your forehead, and write them on the door posts of your house and on your gates" (Deuteronomy 6:4-9).

Again I was blessed this morning to be able to witness a butterfly as he began his new life. What faith the butterfly must have. From a caterpillar, with numerous feet crawling close to the ground, to the beautiful creature of flight, is a big step. As I watch this morning, this butterfly seems to be drying his wings in the morning sun. He rotates around in small circles, then flutters his huge appendages. It's as though he, like everything else, including us, has to learn to be the creature God created him to be.

As a small kitten must learn to hunt and be an adult cat, so it is with most all of life. A mother bird must teach her fledgling to fly. A doe teaches her fawn to blend into the forest for protection. On and on, nature gives examples that forms of life must be taught to reach their potential. I heard someone speak recently concerning the desensitization of our youth today. Because of the senseless and callous crimes that not only youth, but also others, have committed of late, it is as though they have no moral remorse or guilt about their heinous crimes. He went on to say we forget that we must teach our children to become human beings.

Since God created us spirits as well as flesh, we must nurture and guide our spirits, as well as our earthly bodies. Just as we instinctively protect our human bodies from harm, we must also be aware of pitfalls for our spirits. As God was sending signals to that butterfly as to how to dry his wings and begin a life of flight, He will also teach our spirits how to soar. He will convict us of things we're doing to harm our spirits. He will guide and lead us to become the creatures we were created to be. We must allow Him full reign in our lives to tutor us and bring us to our full potential as children of God.

As we protect, feed, and nurture our children, we must always remember also to guide their spirits. We must never neglect the sacred charge that God gave us when he placed them in our care. We must teach them about God. We must sow in their hearts at an early age the awareness and reality of a living and loving God. These are the most important things that we can ever do for our children. We must teach them to be children of God. As the mother bird teaches her young to fly, we must teach them to pray. We must teach them to have a relationship with the Father. Only God can call an individual unto Him, but I do think that parents have a responsibility to lay some of the groundwork. Sow those seeds in your children. God created them as human beings, but it just may be the parents' job to teach them to be humans capable of being children of God.

75

Speedily

"Hear my prayer, O LORD; let my cry come to You. Do not hide Your face from me in the day of my distress. Incline Your ear to me; answer me speedily in the day when I call" (Psalm 102:1-2).

I would venture to say that there are none of us that haven't called out from our distress and wondered why God did not speedily answer our cries. This generation of "I want it now" babies, of whom I am a part, never seemed to develop that pay as you go or patience is a virtue mentality that abounded years ago before credit cards and internet speed. We live in a fast world with fast needs that require fast fixes.

As I watched a mother cardinal training her fledgling this morning at my backyard feeder, I'm reminded of a valuable lesson that God taught me years ago. I've witnessed this teaching scenario many times before. The fledgling, though as big in size as the parent cardinal, stands in her way as she feeds. It calls out its nestling cry for her to feed it. It does the little feed me dance all around her. Though the birdseed is under its feet, the fledgling is still crying out for the nourishment to be poked into its mouth, as it has been since the day it hatched.

I've learned in years past that this is the training period when the fledgling follows the parent to the feeder in order to learn how to live outside the nest on its own. The parent bird finally pokes a seed into the adolescent's mouth and flies off with the fledgling in hot pursuit. I have no idea how long this training goes on before the bird realizes that he is able to fend for himself.

Aren't we much like that fledgling whenever we cry out to God for a speedy answer to our distress? Maybe our faith and past experiences are under our noses like that birdseed. Maybe God has already prepared and equipped us to face this or that trial. Maybe God is trying to teach us an important life lesson from the particular distress in which we find ourselves immersed. Just maybe God is standing afar, not hiding His face from us, but watching as we take those baby steps toward spiritual maturity.

Whatever the scenario, we can be assured that God is there in the distress with us. We can be assured that He does indeed hear our cries. Our answer may not be as speedily as we would like, but God's timing is always perfect. His timing allows for His plans to be met. His timing allows us to grow into that spiritual maturity that one day will lead us home into life everlasting. So if you find yourself in distress, look around and find God. Glean whatever you can from the experience and trust that, "All things" (even distress) "work for the good of those who love the Lord and are called according to His riches and glory" (Romans 8:28). All praise and glory be to our God.

76

Storms

"My brothers and sisters, whenever you face trials of any kind, consider it nothing but joy, because you know that the testing of your faith produces endurance; and let endurance have its full effect, so that you may be mature and complete, lacking in nothing" (James 1:2-4).

Why do we always call the trials and bad things that happen to us in our lives storms? Whenever we seem to be having trouble, we quickly refer to them as ill winds or a storm. As I look out upon everything this morning, I'm aware of last night's storm. The flowers are perky and freshly watered. Everything has freshness to it. Some of the dried leaves of plants have been blown away or broken from the green stems that are newly nourished and full of life. It's as though most everything has benefited from the summer storm.

I've read or heard somewhere that when lightning explodes, there's an oxidizing effect on the air particles around the immediate area. Anyone who has experienced the freshness and newness during or after a storm knows how clean the air smells. The smell of rain on a dry and parched earth has an aroma that saturates and pleases our sense of smell like none other can. We have a spa fragrance called rain that attempts to replicate that wonderful smell. Though it's a pleasing scent, still it cannot compare to the pleasurable smells following a storm.

A storm can quickly eradicate the stale, stagnant air that has weighted us down all day. It can quicken our senses and put us on edge, to experience nature at its most powerful. I remember as a child being so fearful of a storm.

Adults drilled into our heads misconceptions such as noises or dogs attracting lightning. This was their attempt to keep us quiet and keep all other scared critters outside. We had to seek cover and wait out the storm, as though it was something to be feared and endured. At some point in my adulthood, I began to enjoy storms. I'm not naïve enough to stand out in the open or under a tree where lightning is prone to strike, but I do sometimes love to sit under a sheltered porch and experience the awesome power of a storm.

God has let me learn that storms are a good thing to experience instead of the dark, fearful things that I hid from as a child. I no longer need to cover my head or wait out storms. I can embrace and even at times, enjoy them for what they are. Last summer I was blessed to be able to apply this tactic to my illness. I embraced the cancer. This may sound like a strange statement to most. I found that after I had gotten over the initial fear and shock of my diagnosis, God quickly let me know that everything would be all right. I've learned during my Christian journey that all things work for the good of those who love God, just like the Bible tells us. I have grown most after hardships and trials. Like the freshness after the summer storm, I could see where God taught me valuable life lessons during and after the storms in my life.

Developing the mind set that since I was going through this life-threatening storm, I needed to experience the fullness of God's power was a blessing beyond description. I prayerfully searched for all the good that I could glean from this life experience. I was amazed at all the good that did come from it. God made me fresh and new. He pruned away old dried up leaves that I had been fearful or hesitant to sever from my life. He loved me. He oxidized my spirit within me. He empowered me to face this storm with a peace that surpassed all my understanding.

As we each face the storms of our lives, we need to experience and embrace them. Instead of dreading or fearing our life trials, we should consider it nothing but joy, and focus on the one God who will protect us through the storm. We need storms to grow and mature in Christ. Without storms our spirits could possibly become that stale, stagnant air. None of us want to be struck by lightning, but I'm one who has learned that lightning is a necessary natural phenomenon. It refreshes the ozone and oxidizes the air we breathe. I dare to say that just maybe storms are a good thing from God. As long as I can sit under the protected shelter of God the Father, I can enjoy and yes, embrace any storm.

77

The Sunflower

"For everything there is a season, and a time for every matter under heaven: a time to be born, and a time to die; a time to plant, and a time to pluck up what is planted; a time to kill, and a time to heal; a time to break down, and a time to build up; a time to weep, and a time to laugh; a time to mourn, and a time to dance; a time to throw away stones, and a time to gather stones together; a time to embrace, and a time to refrain from embracing; a time to seek, and a time to lose; a time to keep, and a time to throw away; a time to tear, and a time to sew; a time to keep silence, and a time to speak; a time to love, and a time to hate; a time for war, and a time for peace" (Ecclesiastes 3:1-8).

The above Scripture has always been close to my heart. Songs were written about it in the sixties, I've heard many a person quote it when they knew no other Scripture by heart, and it was even included in my mother's funeral eulogy. For everything there is a season, most assuredly. A time for every matter under heaven encompasses all we could ever think about to lift up to God. Recently the eighth verse took on a deeper understanding for me. A time to love and a time to hate are statements so contradictory that I couldn't wrap my mind around them until the sunflower.

One of my daily encounters that became a divine appointment of late was a fellow that I'll call John. John has been on my home delivered meals route for a few years, and he and I have enjoyed many conversations. John is very worldly and a very interesting person to talk to. He's traveled extensively, and quickly he and I bonded by discussing many common interests. I've been blessed to help him on several occasions with little things like doctor appointments and the like. I respect him as a person of value, even though he now is virtually confined to a chair and one small window, through which he can view the vast world that he traveled in younger days.

A few months ago while trying to help John get some much needed assistance that any homebound person has a right to, I discovered John's dark secret. John has no help, friends, or family because he is supposedly guilty of a heinous crime that is abhorred by even me. I was blown away by the uncovering of his past. He was guilty of crimes that would warrant hatred. Was this what the Scripture meant? A time to hate was certainly never more justified. His secret so troubled me that I spent days giving it to God to reconcile my feelings so that I could even go back to see him. I prayed hard and long about my friend. Finally God spoke to me that John's past was for God to handle. John was of no earthly threat to anyone, in his present health state. "Judge not lest ye be judged" (Matthew 7:1), even if it's politically correct to judge such persons in certain instances. Love John was God's command to me. Love him as God loves him, in spite of all his dark past. This was one of the hardest hurdles for me to overcome, and I could only do it through God's grace.

Next God commanded me to pray for John. I had long suspected that John didn't have a personal relationship with God. I began praying diligently that John would accept God as his Lord and Savior. I prayed and prayed, and then one day during a visit, asked John if I might pray with him. "Oh no, I don't want to hear any of that!" was his quick reply as he totally tuned me out. He wasn't ready, and I told him that I wouldn't force anything on him, but that I must let him know that God wanted him to know that God loved him.

I've been careful not to sound preachy or force feed him God's love. God provided a way to show His love that I would never in a million years have come up with. One of my largest and prettiest flowerpots sat under the bird feeder that is in the middle of my decking. As the spring progressed, the most beautiful and healthy sunflower began to emerge from the middle of the potted plants. It shot up toward the sun, in exactly the most perfect section of the pot. Only God could have planted that sunflower where He did. He quickly began to quicken my heart that He had planted that sunflower for John.

"Oh no, God," was my quick response. "Please don't make me give away the most gorgeous pot of flowers that I have out here." Throughout the next week I tried to reason with God and deny that it was Him speaking to me about the sunflower. I didn't want to part with my prize possession. I clung to any thought that justified my keeping the sunflower. How foolish we are when we try to argue with God. I should know by now that surrendering to His will is not always the easiest path, but most certainly the surest path. God's argument was that I had all these other beautiful flowers to enjoy, and John had only what was outside his one window. How selfish I had been to even think about keeping the sunflower.

Needless to say, John enjoyed the sunflower. I dropped by every other day or so to water and feed the prized plant. There are strawberries, sweet Williams, and Johnny jump-ups, also brilliantly blooming beside that divine sunflower. As I water, I hear John tenderly greet me with a "Heeeeey, Sandy." There is most definitely tenderness in his voice. We all know that tenderness is most certainly related to love. Where tenderness lives, love lives, and where love lives, God is granted a doorway. I never miss an opportunity to stick my head inside the door to quickly remind John that God planted that sunflower just for him, because he loves him. He smiles and nods. He won't let me pray with him, but he can't stop God from loving him in spite of rejection. This is the season of John's life to be loved. His health and state of mind let me know that he won't have many more seasons. God wants to love John in this season and I'm so blessed that God allows me to help Him love John. No one should ever have to face death without God, and God is reaching out to John. I know this from my innermost regions. God in His loving mercy is reaching out for even the most wretched, that not one, no not even one, be lost.

As I rewrite this and edit it now, it's been many years since the sunflower and John. John has now gone on to whatever it is that God had prepared for him. Only God knows a man's heart. I trust the God that loved John even when John didn't want to be loved, and has prepared a place for John that just might be filled with sunflowers and all kinds of loving things that will bless John for eternity.

78

Sweet Potato

"But God said to him, 'You fool! This very night your life is being demanded of you. And the things you have prepared, whose will they be? So it is with those who store up treasures for themselves but are not rich toward God'" (Luke 12:20-21).

The first thing I did this morning when I went into the kitchen was to water my sweet potato. A couple of weeks ago I found one of them sprouting out of the eyes and remembered an old scientific experiment we did in grade school. I cut off the five or six inch end, poked four toothpicks in the widest part and balanced it above a glass of water. Just an inch or so of the potato was submerged in the water. Now two weeks later, I have this lush, green foliage growing out of the unsightly base potato. It's beautiful. The darkness and richness of the leaves scream life, health, and vitality. I ponder as I put it back on the shelf, near the florescent light, as to how long it will be before it becomes root bound in the tiny glass.

As I read the Scripture for my upper room, the sweet potato comes immediately to my mind. This is a perfect example of this particular Bible Scripture. To the human eye, this sweet potato appears to be flourishing and growing. In reality, it's only an imitation of the life that a sweet potato should live. I know that in this tiny glass of water it will never grow to bear fruit. All those lovely green leaves can bring all the light and nourishment needed for the potato to grow lots of healthy roots, but, without soil, there will be no new sweet potatoes.

That's exactly how we can live our entire lives. We can be a sweet potato in a glass of water. Unless our spirit is planted deep into the soil of God's power, we cannot bear fruit. We can be wonderfully good people. We can even be Christians that appear to be living the perfect life that leads to heaven. Unless our motives and spirits are centered on Jesus the living Christ, there will be no fruit. A Christian must bear fruit. It's not something we can do on our own. It comes from a close relationship with God the Father. We must store up treasures that are rich toward God and not ourselves. To become selfless as Christ is as essential as that needed soil.

For me, the sweet potato has instantly changed from a scientific experiment into a spiritual example. I know that I'd rather have lots of new potatoes growing from my roots than all the showy green leaves in the world. How easy it is to miss the mark without ever realizing the true way. Plant me in the soil, God, so that I may bear fruit. Though sitting in a glass of water may be quick, comfortable, and easy, plant me deep in the fertile soil where Your blessings abound.

79

Take Your Mat and Walk

"Now in Jerusalem by the Sheep Gate there is a pool, called in Hebrew Bethsaida, which has five porticoes…Jesus said to him, 'Stand up, take your mat and walk'" (John 5:2,8).

I've been there! I've been to that Biblical healing spring of Bethesda, Bethsaida, or Bethzatha. It's beautiful. Many years ago, excavations at the pool of St. Anna in the northeast section of Jerusalem, revealed five porticoes. Today tourists visit this site as the Biblical pool of Bethesda. The porticoes are all dried up now and you must look down into them, but the miracle place still has impact on the spirit.

When we visited this particular site, we also sang inside the church of St. Anna that was adjacent to the pools of Bethesda. Our voices inside that gothic cathedral seemed to spiral all the way up to Heaven. Anyone who has ever visited an ancient gothic cathedral will know exactly what I mean. The structure, with an almost endless ceiling height, seems to catch the human voice and amplify it in such a way that our praises are able to span the vast distance of eternity.

This particular Bible passage tells of the paralyzed man who stayed by the well for thirty-eight years. He had no one to put him in the pool whenever the angel stirred up the healing waters. Someone would always step in front of him and he would miss his healing miracle. You see, the miracle of the pool happened intermittently whenever an angel would flap his wings into the waters and they would bubble for a length of time. Invalids, blind people, lame people, and the paralyzed would rush into the waters as they bubbled, in order to receive their healing.

Our guide explained that excavations had shown that movement of the water was probably caused by an underground spring, which would have stirred up the waters enough, on occasion, to make them mysteriously bubble. Modern man had explained away another of the Bible's miraculous mysteries. For a time I was satisfied with our guide's explanation, which had made this Scripture logical and understandable to my way of thinking.

Deeper thought and the Holy Spirit's understanding allow me to see the real miracle. The fact is that people were healed at the pools of Bethesda. The fact is that whether miracle waters, angels, or sheer faith were the reason, people were healed. Jesus showed the paralyzed man that it wasn't necessary to get into the waters, but that he need only believe that he was healed and he could walk.

This same miracle is afforded to each of us yet today, over 2000 years later. We need not step into the healing waters. We need only to believe in the one great Physician's healing powers. Believing in His power to overcome any obstacle we may face is the real miracle. We can spend thirty-eight years or our entire lives lying on a mat beside the waters, waiting, or we can look into the face of Jesus, take up our mat and walk. The choice is ours. The real miracle again is simply in believing.

Those miracle healing pools take many forms in our lives today. We can spend much of our lives waiting for this or waiting for that particular thing to happen, in order for our lives to be made whole. The miracle is that we need to take disciplined action concerning our unnamed need. We must believe! We must believe that we can do all things through Him who strengthens us and let Jesus work his miracle healing powers in us. It's as accessible today as it was way back then during the paralytic's time. Jesus is saying, "Stand up, take your mat and walk."

80

Butterfly

"He said to them, 'Because of your little faith. For truly I tell you, if
you have faith the size of a mustard seed, you will say to this mountain, 'Move from here to there,' and it will move; and nothing will
be impossible for you'" (Matthew 17:20-21).

Can you imagine how much faith a butterfly must have? As I watched
a newly emerged butterfly slowly move his wings in the morning sun, this question crossed my mind. He seemed to be drying out his wings in the morning
sun. He turned 360 degrees, flapping ever so often as to catch the sun's rays.
Can we even fathom what may be running through that little butterfly's mind?
(Assuming they have thoughts.)

He's spent all his waking hours crawling. Crawling along the blades
of grass. Maybe he even crawled as high as a tree branch to make his cocoon.
Then, he slept for whatever time was allotted him to sleep. All he has ever
known was the sure-footed journey of solid ground beneath his weight. What
a shock when the multiple footed caterpillar awakes to find two huge wings at-
tached to his back. I feel sure that "off balance" doesn't begin to describe what
he would feel.

While I watch him try his wings the first time, I think that he must have
taken the proverbial leap of faith. To go from crawling on many legs to soaring
on two wings would have to take all the faith he could muster.

As I crawl and creep through my spiritual journey with God, I sometimes am asked to do things that I don't feel comfortable doing. I drag my feet
and try to reason with God that I'm not ready or not able to tackle whatever He
may be convicting me to do. How foolish such a conversation with God is!

191

Of course, I'm not able! Only God is able. He will empower us to do whatever He calls us to do. Our ability isn't a factor. He can change our caterpillar feet into butterfly wings. All things are possible with God. If we could only have the faith of a small butterfly, what miracles God could work through each and every one of us.

81

The Darkness Does Not Overcome

"In the beginning was the Word, and the Word was with God, and the Word was God. He was in the beginning with God. All things came into being through Him, and without Him not one thing came into being. What has come into being in Him was life and the life was the light of all people. The light shines in the darkness, and the darkness did not overcome it" (John 1:1-5).

As I read God's Word this morning, I am overwhelmed by the power in these few verses of John. Wow! God was the Word, and the Word was with God! All things came into being through Him...life...and the life was the light of all the people. The light shines in the darkness, and the darkness did not overcome it.

It's 6:00 AM and still pitch dark outside. As I look out the side window, I spy the small lights flashing on a tower a few miles away. The light flashes in a pulsing rhythm into the darkness. It strikes a cord inside of me like never before.

At times my life feels like the darkness that engulfs that one little blinking light. Especially on one of these sleepless nights, it's as though the weight of the world or darkness could, at any moment, simply snuff out my little light.

The constant battle of disease and old age against the life and breath within me sometimes overwhelms me with fear and anxiety. What keeps a Christian going at a time like this? The Word! The Word of God! "The Word was with God and the Word was God" (John 1:1). Complete immersion in the Word will without a doubt brighten our small, sometimes wavering light.

God promises that the darkness will not overcome the light. As I feed on God's Word, I can expect my light to brighten and pierce through any darkness. Darkness is evil and fear is darkness; therefore, fear and evil are synonymous. In order for darkness not to overcome light, I must, therefore, fear no evil.

As I focus now, not on the darkness, but on that small, beckoning light, I am reminded that Jesus came as the light of the world to save us from the darkness. Through Him, I can release all fears of the night and walk with Him in the light assured of God's life in the Word. As the dawning light of the rising sun begins to spread across the horizon, the little blinking light that I've been watching begins to fade. Then I realize that indeed the darkness cannot overcome my light, but, that the light of Jesus Christ can absorb my small light and drive away all darkness, fear, anxiety, and evil.

82

The Hibiscus

"I am the vine, you are the branches. Those who abide in me and I in them bear much fruit, because apart from me you can do nothing. Whoever does not abide in me is thrown away like a branch and withers; such branches are gathered, thrown into the fire, and burned. If you abide in me, and my words abide in you, ask for whatever you wish, and it will be done for you. My Father is glorified by this, that you bear much fruit and become my disciples. As the Father has loved me, so I have loved you; abide in my love. If you keep my commandments, you will abide in my love, just as I have kept my Father's commandments and abide in His love. I have said these things to you so that my joy may be in you, and that your joy may be complete" (John 15:5-11).

I learned a valuable lesson from the hibiscus in my yard. The more mature plant was a pale, pale pink while the newer plant was a luscious, vivid pink. I pondered on this and wondered why there was such a difference in color. The newer plant had been transplanted from the older one, so they should have the same genetic makeup. Why would the newer look brilliant, while the older look faded?

Maybe the older, more mature plant didn't need the bright blooms to attract flying insects. After all, it was healthy and well established with a good root system and lots of green foliage. The newer, younger plant was only about one fifth the size of the parent plant. Those bright, pink blossoms would have to take it a long, long way to catch up with the larger hibiscus. Then this thought struck me. Do we as mature Christians rest in our salvation and the Lord's grace? Do we take nourishment from our well-established root system and fail to blossom as brilliantly and brightly as when we were new in our walk with God?

As a baby Christian, I recall being excited and ready for whatever God asked me to do. I was confident, and still am, in His grace to empower me to do His will. I find myself guilty of not always acting on the things of which God convicts me. I do know that resting in my faith is essential to my spiritual well being. Even Jesus went off by Himself to rest and get away from the crowds. I must admit that the older and more tired I become, I find myself resting a bit too much.

Although those huge, pale, pink blossoms are extremely beautiful, those bright, vivid pink ones seem to me to be more attractive. As we mature Christians bear fruit, is our fruit pale, pristine, and lovely to look at, or is it bright, luscious, and inviting? Does our fruit attract people to the Lord, Jesus Christ; does it make His grace seem cool, private, and unattainable? We have a wonderful, God-given root system. We are empowered to bear vivid, exciting, brilliant fruit! Opportunities are out there and doors are wide open. May we all unfold our petals and bloom magnetic blossoms that draw souls to our Lord.

83

Nativity

"… to you is born this day in the city of David a Savior, who is the Messiah, the Lord. This will be a sign for you: you will find a child wrapped in bands of cloth and lying in a manger" (Luke 2:11-12).

As I pray this morning for God to create in me a clean and right heart in order to worship Him this Christmas, my focus is turned toward my display of nativities in the window seat. Most years, I put out on display many nativity sets that I've collected through the years. Some years, I only put out a couple, then other years, I get industrious and put out as many as twenty or so in a shrine-like display in my window seat. This year, I'm drawn over to the display and ponder on each and every one of the seventeen scenes depicted in this array of Christmas time.

As my gaze jumps from one to another, I marvel at the diversity in these numerous renditions of Jesus' birth. They vary in composition. Some are crystal, some porcelain, some plastic, some are olivewood from Jerusalem, and one is even made from native soapstone in Panama. They also vary in numbers present at that holiest of nights. From as few as three, consisting of Joseph, Mary, and baby Jesus, to as many as eleven, including animals, wisemen, shepherds, and angels. I think to myself, Jesus is so diversified that He might answer the need of all peoples, everywhere.

Then, just as quickly, another thought strikes me! Instead of the differences in the sets, I realize the one thing they have in common. All of the tiny or large figurines have their focus on the baby Jesus that is the center of each display. Even the animals are made so that bowed heads gaze upon the tiny Wonder lying in each manger scene. The heads of the wisemen are bowed in adoration. The shepherds are coming toward the holy trough with their eyes on its precious contents.

How marvelous that all these many artisans from various places could capture the true essence of Christmas. Our focus should be on the central focus of this holy night. The Messiah, Immanuel, the Christ Child, baby Jesus should be all that we consider during this season for mankind. Forget the hustle, forget the gift buying, forget the conflicting family schedules, or any other thing that might distract us from focusing on the one constant miracle.

He came that we might have life more abundant. He came that we might have life everlasting. He came that we might know the true essence of love for our fellow man. Christmas isn't about anything but God's love for mankind. His gift to us should outweigh any thought we might entertain about the true meaning of Christmas.

"For God so loved the world that He gave His only begotten Son" (John 3:16), should ring from the highest mountaintop. We are celebrating not only the birth of the Christ Child. We are celebrating God's love for us. His unfathomable love that is poured out to us each and every day is somehow more apparent during this holy season. As we soak in that love, we can be filled to overflowing and spill out onto our fellow man. This is the true focus and essence of Christmas!

84

The Next Room

"Happy are the people to whom such blessings fall; happy are the people whose God is the LORD" (Psalms 144:15).

I'm remembering another spring day today on this beautiful day that the Lord has made. It was a few years ago when I used to volunteer at an area hospital. I volunteered in patient services. I would take ice, water, cards, and flowers to patients. On occasion, it was very difficult to go to the hospital and give an afternoon that I could otherwise be enjoying outside or doing something for myself. This was just such a day! It was one of the first days of spring. The sun, the flowers, the birds all screamed at my spirit to get outside and enjoy them. I prayed harder on the way to the hospital that God would bless me for the time I was willing to give up in order to serve Him. Wow! Did He ever bless me!

I did all the duties that I normally had to do and was on my way to the patient's rooms. This volunteer situation had daily rewards. To spark a smile or a friendly banter from a patient, who would otherwise be having a low day, always lifted my spirits more than theirs. As I came to a very darkened room, I remember thinking, Pour on the charm, this person is really having a bad day. I remember saying something to the effect of, "Why in the world do you have your drapes closed on such a beautiful spring day?"

I was left nearly speechless when the reply, "Ma'am, I'm blind," came back at me. God was with me because I never missed a beat. I swept over to the window, pulled back the drapes and began to describe everything my eyes came to. I went into detail about the dogwoods that were in bloom, the crocus and tulips that were coming up in the flowerbeds outside his window. There was a bird building a nest in a nearby tree. He got a detailed description of the world going on outside his window. He sat silently with tears in his eyes. As I got ready to leave, he thanked me over and over for taking the time to describe everything so vividly. My heart swelled as I felt the pure joy that God blesses us with when we are in His will for us. I was mentally thanking God for this wonderful blessing and thought that my cup was full of joy until I reached the next room.

Standing in the doorway of the next room was a woman crying like a baby. As I approached her, she came toward me saying, "Please let me hug you." I didn't know what to think, but willingly obliged her. As we hugged there in the doorway, she explained to me that she had spent the last two days at her dying mother's bedside. Her mother's serious state had left her distraught and depressed. When she had heard me at the doorway of the blind man's room, she had leaned against her doorway, closed her eyes, and listened.

She said my descriptions had been so very beautiful that had_she not been able to see, she could have imagined the spring day in her mind. Wow! God, you are such an awesome God! Here, I had thought that He had been using me to bless the blind man in the other room, and all the while, I was blessing the lady in the next room. The appreciation of the spring day had brought a ray of sunshine into her day. She explained that she had hurried to her mother's side that morning, without taking the time to thank God for the beautiful spring day. For just a few moments, God had taken her out of her situation and been able to love and comfort her.

My heart swelled even more. I thought of the saying I had heard years ago, "My cup runneth over and I've been drinking out of the saucer for years." Today definitely had been one of those saucer days for me. What pure joy we experience, when we surrender ourselves totally to the will of God. I learned long ago that whenever I dread giving Him my time the most, I can expect the most reward for my effort. I thank you, Lord, and pray that you continue letting me go into that next room.

85

There is a City

"There is a river whose streams make glad the city of God, the holy habitation of the Most High. God is in the midst of the city; it shall not be moved; God will help it when the morning dawns. The nations are in an uproar, the kingdoms totter; He utters His voice, the earth melts. The LORD of hosts is with us; the God of Jacob is our refuge. Come behold the works of the LORD; see what desolation He has brought on the earth. He makes wars cease to the end of the earth; He breaks the bow, and shatters the spear; He burns the shields with fire. 'Be still, and know that I am God'" (Psalm 46:4-10)!

I dare to say that not many of us today know what it's like, not to live in or near a city! I was born and raised a country girl down on the farm. We farmed and raised tobacco. We played cowboys with stick horses. We pretended to chew tobacco and spit like a cowboy should, with the aid of a sour, green apple that made the driest mouth salivate. We dipped snuff made of cocoa and sugar. We chewed on a dogwood snuff brush, much like Great Grandma chewed.

I spent most of my summer days climbing the old walnut tree beside Grandma's house, building stringed play houses in the woods, and enjoying a simpler life filled with imagination. An extra special day would find me making a skirt of leaves and playing Sheena, queen of the jungle, as I swung through the woods on a wild grapevine. Tying a string to a June bug or horned tobacco worm gave me hours and hours of enjoyment. Singing to doodlebugs buried under a mound of red dirt and making hoppy toad houses with mud over my little foot filled day after day of my childhood.

Life in the country is the absolute other end of the spectrum when compared to life in a city. A city is filled with people. Where there are too many people, we find traffic jams, long lines, tempers flaring and the rush and madness of too much haste. We must prepare, we must wrap, and we must attend party after party. A city during the Christmas season becomes a mecca for hurried shoppers, last minute preparations, and more often than not, a lethal weapon that kills the true intent of what Christmas is all about.

This passage today describes a city like I've never seen. It describes a city beyond any of my personal experiences of a city. To picture this city I must go back to my childhood and utilize that imagination that I enjoyed so well. Christmastime takes us back to the city of David. The small city of Bethlehem is where it all began. The Messiah came to us in that city of long ago. I've seen that quaint little town that is also called a city. But, this Scripture is speaking of a city beyond that holy city. It's speaking of that city to come.

There is a city to come that will fulfill all our greatest desires. It will be a city of eternal peace. There will be no wars, no rush, no sin, no pain, no worries, nothing that would ever mar our perfect happiness and peace. That holy city of God is real. Imagine what it would be like to never cry, to never hurt, to never do anything but worship, praise, and love. Our God is a mighty God. He's prepared just such a place for us whenever we leave this world. And yet, He allows us an imagination to experience a glimpse of it now, today, here in this life. We simply must stop in the midst of all the turmoil going on around us. In the very midst of your holiday preparations and haste, be still and know that He is God. My quiet moment just took me to a place that I had not visited in many years, my childhood.

Be still, be still and allow God to quiet your very soul. This season is not simply preparation after preparation after preparation. If you allow that to happen, soon it will be over and you will have missed it. I've had that happen and wondered why I had been so busy making preparations. Be still and allow God to visit you this holiest of seasons. He will, you know. He's always there to allow you a glimpse of that holy city to come. You simply need to be still and allow Him access to your often too busy life. "Glory to God in the Highest and on earth, peace and goodwill toward men" (Luke 2:14).

86

The Whole Shell

"I am astonished that you are so quickly deserting the one who called you in the grace of Christ and are turning to a different gospel — not that there is another gospel, but there are some who are confusing you and want to pervert the gospel of Christ. But even if we or an angel from Heaven should proclaim to you a gospel contrary to what we proclaimed to you, let that one be accursed! As we have said before, so now I repeat, if anyone proclaims to you a gospel contrary to what you received, let that one be accursed! Am I now seeking human approval, or God's approval? Or am I trying to please people? If I were still pleasing people, I would not be a servant of Christ. For I want you to know, brothers and sisters, that the gospel that was proclaimed by me is not of human origin; for I did not receive it from a human source, nor was I taught it, but I received it through a revelation of Jesus Christ" (Galatians 1:6-12).

We just spent the most wonderful vacation by the seashore. Glorious days of sun, fun, and mostly relaxation were our only agenda. As I reflect back on the past ten days respite, the memory of my three-year-old granddaughter's first experience of the seashore comes to mind.

We can see pictures, television programs, and vivid descriptions of the ocean's sandy beaches, but none of them can come close to the experience of that first visit to the seashore. How can we begin to describe that humbling feeling in the pit of our stomachs as we experience one of God's most awesome creations? The sheer helplessness of the frail human as he stands beside the vastness of the pounding surf makes us aware of God's power. Humbling, awe inspiring, and just plain wonderment are things that come to my mind.

As my little granddaughter discovered that the sand was full of little collectable seashells, her amazement heightened. She must have inherited my love of shells. She started running from one shell fragment to the next. "Nana, we have to get them all," she gulped in her excitement. Knowing that I would have to carry the mesh bag of shells, I was quick to explain to her that we couldn't possibly get them all. We should be selective and try to collect only the "whole" shells. Of course since this was her first encounter with shells, she couldn't recognize which were whole and which were mere fragments.

Memories of her collecting shells came to my mind as I read Paul's address to the Galatians this morning. I'm one who loves to watch Christian television. God long ago revealed to me that I could glean bits and pieces from hosts of speakers and preachers to get the whole gospel. Some evangelists focus on one aspect while other preachers zero in elsewhere. We should never let ourselves be content with fragments of the gospel.

God uses His people as He sees fit. What He reveals through one servant, another servant may not focus on. He networks and uses those who will allow Him access to their lives. I liken our different denominations to the shell fragments. Man foolishly focuses on the fragment that speaks to him instead of looking for the whole shell. We all have a responsibility to baby Christians to help them recognize the whole shell or truth.

I tried to explain to my little granddaughter what were whole shells and which were fragments. We as Christians should always point our new brothers and sisters in Christ to the whole shell. Jesus the Christ is the whole gospel, and the good news. He may be offered up as a different gospel as Paul speaks of in the above Scripture. Be assured that if we accept Jesus Christ as the whole gospel, He will reveal Himself to us. We won't have to please people. What is politically correct is not always Biblically correct! Allow the one true Christ to reveal Himself to you that you might share the whole gospel with others.

87

Why Parables?

"With them indeed is fulfilled the prophecy of Isaiah that says: 'You will indeed listen, but never understand, and you will indeed look, but never perceive. For this people's heart has grown dull, and their ears are hard of hearing, and they have shut their eyes; so that they might not look with their eyes, and listen with their ears, and understand with their heart and turn — and I would heal them.' But blessed are your eyes, for they see, and your ears, for they hear. Truly I tell you, many prophets and righteous people longed to see what you see, but did not see it, and to hear what you hear, but did not hear it" (Matthew 13:14-17).

This Scripture relays Jesus' answer to the apostles whenever they questioned him as to why He spoke in parables. Why did He? I've heard many wonderful people ask the same thing. Why did He speak of seeds, sowers, sheep, and shepherds? He told stories that were simple for the simple man of the day. He told stories to people whose livelihood was in shepherding. He told stories to farmers who knew the principles of seedtime and harvest. He spoke over no one's head. He came to include the simplest of men into the heights of understanding God's glory. Only man's high-mindedness or hardheartedness kept him from understanding Jesus' simple parables.

He spoke of families and relationships. He spoke of forgiveness and love. He spoke to any that would listen in the plain and simple language of the day. He was unlike the Pharisees and Saducees, who spoke with the language of the Torah. He was the Torah made flesh. He was the law in the form of man that we might see the Torah fulfilled. He was the very image of His Father God. He made our adoption possible so that we might grow that seed He implanted in us to become children of that same living God.

What a blessing this week's revival has been. This pastor is most definitely is anointed by God to teach. Though his title is preacher/doctor, he is first and foremost a teacher. This world needs fewer preachers and more teachers. Think about it, Jesus was more times than not referred to as teacher, not preacher. He came to teach us the divine nature of God. He came to put those Torah laws into layman's terms. He spoke in parables in order to reach the least, the last, and the lost.

We must nurture our relationship with Jesus and let Him teach us the way, the truth, and the light. The Church of Jesus the Christ is a wondrous and beautiful thing. He left instructions for the Church. He is coming back for His Church. His Church is of one mind and one heart. His Church will consist of simple people from all religions and all creeds who understand His truth and His way. His church will not be made of wood, bricks, or block walls. We must strive to be His bride, the Church. His Church consists of people. His Church will be people who have eyes and ears that are blessed to see and hear. He's coming back for His Church who's hearts have not grown dull, deaf, or blind.

Why parables; why not? I know that whenever Jesus speaks to me today, He speaks so that I can understand Him. Oh, sure once in a while, He may throw out a little of that King James language to me, but, all in all, He speaks that I might understand and grow in my relationship with Him. The parables are beautiful stories that have much import and meaning to us, yet today. Sharpen your eyes, ears and hearts to His messages found in the parables that are still so current to our lives. That seed has been planted in you. Nurture it. Grow it. Feed it with the living waters and the fire of the Holy Spirit. Grow, brothers and sisters, grow!

88

Wind in Your Sails

"Jesus answered, 'Very truly I tell you, no one can enter the kingdom of God without being born of water and Spirit. What is born of the flesh is flesh, and what is born of the Spirit is spirit. Do not be astonished that I said to you, 'You must be born from above.' The wind blows where it chooses, and you hear the sound of it, but you do not know where it comes from or where it goes. So it is with everyone who is born of the Spirit'" (John 3:5-8).

As the soft breeze brushes my cheek this morning, the above Scripture comes to mind. I can remember someone once saying that the translation for wind in this particular Scripture should have been Spirit. That would have relayed to us that the Spirit blows where it chooses. Since hearing that, I always close my eyes when the wind kisses my cheek and visualize the Spirit of God, physically touching me with a comforting caress that reassures me of God's loving care. It's a sensation that originates in the spiritual realm and transcends to the physical realm for me. It's a sweet gift that always stops me in my tracks so that I might relish the sensation. As the Scripture states, we can hear the sound of it and even feel the touch of it, but not see from whence it comes or where it goes. I personally feel that a gentle breeze is just one of God's mysteries.

A gentle breeze can become a strong wind that will move a huge sailing ship across the vast waters of the oceans. I've seen movies with those majestic sailing ships adorned with billowy sails. How beautiful they are when the winds feed those sails and move that mighty vessel. The ship, when standing still with no wind in its sails, isn't nearly as beautiful or powerful as the one being moved along the waves with a good wind. Our life can often be compared to that beautiful sailing ship.

We've all had sin, sickness, death, or some other trial in life come along to knock the wind out of our sails. We can sit heavy, laden, and motionless in the waters of life, much like that ship without winds to feed its sails. Burdened with our load, we are impotent to move through the waters of life. Then just as this Scripture tells us, from we know not where, comes the wind (Spirit) to feed our sails and continue us on along our way. Those born of the Spirit will never be set adrift for long. We are assured of this through Scripture after Scripture. Our God will never forsake us. He is steadfast and sure.

Christians must always remember that we are no longer flesh but spirit. Our God will always send His Spirit to fill our sails for the passage through life. Those sails will never be drooping for long. As soon as we get our focus back upon the God who will fill us, our sails will billow as never before. As majestic and beautiful as those old sailing vessels, we will be along our way filled with the Spirit of God that knows no defeat. Our God is greater than any trial that we might face. Fill us, dear Lord; fill us with the Holy Spirit from the God we have chosen to serve. Put the wind in our sails and send us along our way. Your will be done.

89

Words

"…I pray that, according to the riches of His glory, He may grant that you may be strengthened in your inner being with power through His Spirit, and that Christ may dwell in your hearts through faith… " (Ephesians 3:14-21).

I love words! They fascinate me. Whenever a word catches my attention, I love to consider all its different meanings and uses. Some words can be nouns as well as verbs. I find it amazing that we can use the same word to name an object and then turn around and use it to describe some action. The above Scripture is one of my favorites. I refer back to it often. I have a note written in the margin of my Bible beside the highlighted scripture, reminding me that it gives me peace and that it's a beautiful blessing.

Faith is one of those double definition words. Faith must be the foundation of someone's entire relationship with God. I have learned somewhere that in Greek or Hebrew, faith is also a verb. A verb, as we all know, is a word of action. We must continually faith in our relationship with God. This word may very well be one of those double-edged swords that the Bible speaks of in Hebrews 4:12. It can be used as a tool, as well as be enjoyed as a blessing. In order to have faith the noun, we must faith the verb. I find it fascinating! We can't simply rest on the faith we've already been blessed to obtain, we must continue to faith. It's a continual ongoing growth process as we journey with God. The more faith we obtain, the more faith we are able to utilize in our lives.

Another part of this Scripture is … Christ may dwell in your hearts through faith. Dwell is another one of those words that I find interesting. It is used abundantly throughout Bible Scripture. Dwell is a word that is easily overlooked. Dwell means to live in. A word's definition doesn't always give us a clue to its original root word or words. Dwell appears to me to have come from an obvious contraction of the two words, do and well. We would do well to have Christ living or dwelling on the inside of us.

God gave us the Bible as a road map to live our lives. The Bible is a book of words. These words come from God and have many meanings. The living Word can take on many meanings, depending on what state of mind or what particular circumstance we may be in at the time of its reading. I personally think this is why it can be called the living Word, because it is constantly changing to adapt to our particular needs. Though God is the same yesterday, today, and forever, God uses multi-faceted words to reach us in our worldly state and humanly form. He also sends the Holy Spirit to interpret those words. As we read His word, we should always be open to the Holy Spirit to help us understand the meaning that God is trying to convey to us. Dig deep into the words and ponder their meanings. Spend time in the Word.

I am fascinated by words, but I am in awe of The Word. I know that God didn't speak into a dictaphone, and Moses, the prophets, and the followers of Christ were not like stenographers, typing every word. I do believe by faith that every word was inspired by the living God who is the Word and dwells in me. We need only to open ourselves to God, open our Bibles and His living Word will speak to us. Again, dig into the living Word, dig deeply and find whatever tool or double-edged sword God wants you to wield today!

Time Spent With God

About the Author

Sandy Blackburn

Sandy Blackburn is a stay-at-home wife and grandmother raising her oldest grandchild. As an active volunteer in her church and small rural community of Welcome, North Carolina, she makes her quiet time with God a daily priority in her busy life. Writing and lay speaking have allowed her opportunities to use all the broken and shattered fragments of her life into devotionals and messages that encourage others and glorify God. From losing her first child to the ultimate loss of three young granddaughters in a horrible car accident, she has experienced first-hand the faithfulness of a loving and most gracious God.

To schedule Sandy for speaking engagements,
revivals, retreats or booksignings, contact:

Sandy Blackburn
Lexington, NC 27295
Phone 336-731-2241
Email: koolpools@triad.rr.com

213

the Hoppers
america's favorite family of gospel music

With humble beginnings as rural farm-boys, The Hoppers (originally known as the Hopper Brothers and Connie) were formed in 1957 by founding member and owner, Claude Hopper. The group, green in experience, consisted of Claude, his four brothers Will, Steve, Paul and Monroe, and his future wife, Connie. Over the years, the Hopper Brothers and Connie welcomed and then parted with musicians and singers who have gone on to their acclaimed service in Christian music. Connie and Claude's two sons, Dean and Michael, eventually joined the group full-time as lead vocalist and drummer. In 1981, The Hoppers were chosen to represent the genre of Southern Gospel Music at the Religious Inaugural Celebration for President Ronald Reagan.

While The Hoppers achieved tremendous success through the first three decades of ministry, the era of the '90s began a new leg of their journey with the addition of Dean's wife, Kim, as soprano and a streak of hit number one songs including: "Milk and Honey", "Here I Am", "Anchor to the Power of the Cross", and " Mention My Name".

The pace of the group, with God's help, was hitting new strides. In addition to radio success, The Hoppers have received numerous accolades including Mixed Group of the Year from the Heart's Aflame Awards, Diamond Awards, Singing News Fan Awards, and the SGMA; as well as four Dove Award nominations. In 1998, Connie was presented with the prestigious Marvin Norcross award, which is given to those with excellence in "Devotion to family, service to Church, and contributions to the Gospel Music Industry". Michael received the Musician of the Year award from the Singing News Fan Awards, along with Kim who has had the privilege of being given the title of Female Vocalist and Favorite Soprano for well over a decade by the same association.

The Hoppers have been traveling the country, and more recently, the world spreading the Gospel while performing fan favorites like "Jerusalem", "Yes I Am", "Shoutin' Time", "Yaweh", "The Ride", and "Blame it on Love".

The group has always tried to remain stalwart in their sharing of hope and God's unmatchable love, while keeping their faith in Christ and family. Their prayer is to extend this message to *all* who do not know Him, and encourage *all* who do.

w w w . t h e h o p p e r s . c o m

Join Us. Become Involved.

The Hopper Heritage Foundation is a non-profit organization solely dedicated to encouraging, supporting and celebrating Southern Gospel music and contributing to the education of a new generation of Christian leaders.

We encourage you and your family to become actively involved in the Hopper Heritage Foundation through your time and tax-deductible donations. By working together, we can protect the musical heritage of Southern Gospel music, and assure the continuance of the life-changing Gospel message in song for future generations.

You Can Make Your Tax-Deductible Donations to:

Hopper Heritage Foundation

811 US HWY 220
Madison, NC 27025
(336) 548-2968
FAX (336) 548-4288
Email: heritage@thehoppers.com
www.hopperheritagefoundation.org

Other Inspiring Titles

By Woodland Gospel Publishing
AN IMPRINT OF WOODLAND PRESS, LLC

After All These Years

The Authorized Biography of The Hoppers

By F. Keith Davis
Foreword: Dr. John Hagee
Introduction: Dr. Charles F. Stanley

This is the biography of America's Favorite Family of Gospel Music, the Hoppers. It's the account of the longtime anchors of the Gaither Homecoming videos, television shows and concerts. The Hoppers are award-winning Gospel Music artists. Inside this book, there are many rare and personal photos of the family from their beginnings in 1957 to today. Over the years they have experienced many mountaintop experiences and have faced just as many tragic valleys. Regardless, this American family has established a Southern Gospel Music legacy over the last half-century. They also have an inspiring story to tell. *After All These Years, the Authorized Biography of the Hoppers* is their story. Hardcover. $24.99

Available at www.thehoppers.com

What's My Excuse

For Not Being A Christian

By Brad Crouser

Distinguished author and attorney Brad Crouser explains that to many of this age, the Christian gospel message is considered "foolishness." To them it's not a respectable or credible philosophy. It's something only uneducated, unsophisticated, easily lead, gullible people would accept. However, the Apostle Paul quotes God's pronouncement in Isaiah 29:14, "I will destroy the wisdom of the wise; the intelligence of the intelligent I will frustrate." The gospel might be foolishness to "those who are perishing," Paul writes, "but to us who are being saved it is the power of God."

This project is unique. Brad is not a theologian. He did not attend a seminary. As he describes this work, it is a "lay" book, written by a "layman," developed for others without a formal Bible education. Inside this volume, Brad tackles a dozen of the most common myths about the Christian life.

As Brad best explains it inside the volume, "If you're looking for light reading with amusing anecdotes, I'm sorry — this is probably not for you. We're going to discuss some serious business here. Issues of eternal consequence." Softcover. $13.95

Available at www.woodlandpress.com

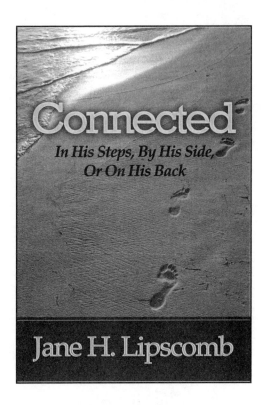

Connected

In His Steps, By His Side, or On His Back

By Jane H. Lipscomb

This new volume, Connected: In His Steps, By His Side, or On His Back, is a wonderful literary triumph. It's designed to acquaint the reader with poignant and powerful glimpses into intimacy with the Heavenly Father. Along the way, meet author Jane Heinz Lipscomb. She is a mother, grandmother, great-grandmother, businesswoman, accomplished pianist, teacher and speaker—but, above all, she's a vibrant word artist who can transport anyone .... effortlessly.

The result of Connected: In His Steps, By His Side, or On His Back, is the creation of an inspiring devotional that will take you on a powerful and life-changing journey. A fine work that should be in every inspirational library. Softcover. $15.95

Woodland Press, LLC